ABE LINCOLN GROWS UP

By

CARL SANDBURG

Reprinted from Abraham Lincoln: The Prairie Years
With illustrations by
JAMES DAUGHERTY

Harcourt Brace & Company
San Diego   New York   London

Library of Congress Cataloging-in-Publication Data
Sandburg, Carl, 1878–1967.
Abe Lincoln grows up.
1. Lincoln, Abraham, Pres. U.S., 1809–1865.
I. Title.
E457.3.S23   1975   973.7′092′4[B]   74-17180
ISBN 0-15-201037-8
ISBN 0-15-602615-5 pb

Printed in the United States of America

T   V   X   Z   AA   Y   W   U

Publisher's Note

Carl Sandburg's "*Abraham Lincoln, the Prairie Years,*" was first published for Lincoln's birthday, 1926. Since then it has become increasingly evident that the book lives for people of all ages and kinds; but the later chapters on Lincoln's political life are of necessity less interesting for boy and girl readers of today than the earlier ones about his own boyhood.

This book is made from the first twenty-seven chapters of the original two-volume biography. James Daugherty has drawn the illustrations. As he says, "*Out of certain special individual experiences and affections vivified and roused by this book—memories of my own early boyhood in Southern Ohio and Indiana—endeavor has sprung to embellish the pages of this noble story.*"

Here we have Lincoln's babyhood and boyhood at Knob Creek Farm and on Little Pigeon Creek; his games and chores; the things he handles and uses; his life at Gentryville and on the Mississippi; until at nineteen, leaving home to make his fortune at New Salem, "*Abe Lincoln Grows Up.*"

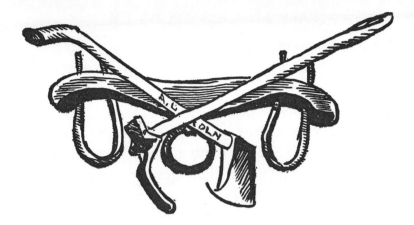

CHAPTER I

In the year 1776, when the thirteen American colonies of England gave to the world that famous piece of paper known as the Declaration of Independence, there was a captain of Virginia militia living in Rockingham County, named Abraham Lincoln.

He was a farmer with a 210-acre farm deeded to him by his father, John Lincoln, one of the many English, Scotch, Irish, German, Dutch settlers who were taking the green hills and slopes of the Shenandoah Valley and putting their plows to ground never touched with farming tools by the red men, the Indians, who had held it for thousands of years.

The work of driving out the red men so that the white

men could farm in peace was not yet finished. In the summer of that same year of 1776, Captain Abraham Lincoln's company took a hand in marches and fights against the Cherokee tribes.

It was a time of much fighting. To the south and west were the red men. To the north and east were white men, the regiments of British soldiers, and Virginia was sending young men and corn and pork to the colonial soldiers under General George Washington. Amos Lincoln, a kinsman of Abraham, up in Massachusetts, was one of the white men who, the story ran, rigged out as Indians, went on board a British ship and dumped a cargo of tea overboard to show their disobedience, contempt, and defiance of British laws and government; later Amos was a captain of artillery in the colonial army.

There was a Hananiah Lincoln who fought at Brandywine under Washington and became a captain in the Twelfth Pennsylvania regiment; and Hananiah was a first cousin of Abraham. Jacob Lincoln, a brother of Abraham, was at Yorktown, a captain under Washington at the finish of the Revolutionary War. These Lincolns in Virginia came from Berks County in Pennsylvania.

Though they were fighting men, there was a strain of Quaker blood running in them; they came in part from people who wore black clothes only, used the word "thee"

[4]

instead of "you," kept silence or spoke "as the spirit of the heart moved," and held war to be a curse from hell; they were a serene, peaceable, obstinate people.

Now Abraham Lincoln had taken for a wife a woman named Bathsheba Herring. And she bore him three sons there amid the green hills and slopes of the Shenandoah Valley, and they were named Mordecai, Josiah, and Thomas. And she bore two daughters, named Mary and Nancy.

This family of a wife and five children Abraham Lincoln took on horses in the year 1782 and moved to Kentucky. For years his friend, Daniel Boone, had been coming back from trips to Kentucky, sometimes robbed of all his deerskins and bearskins and furs of fox and mink, sometimes alone and without the lusty young bucks who had started with him for Kentucky. And listening to Boone's telling of how the valleys were rich with long slopes of black land and blue grass, how there were game and fish, and tall timber and clear running waters—and seeing the road near his farm so often filled with parties of men and families headed for the wilderness beyond the mountains—he began thinking about taking up land for himself over there. It was his for forty cents an acre. He wanted to be where he could look from his cabin to the horizons on all sides—and the land all his own—was that it? He didn't know. It called to him, that country Boone was talking about.

Boone and his friends had worn a trail following an old buffalo path down the Shenandoah Valley to Lexington

and around to Cumberland Gap in Tennessee, then north-west into Kentucky. It had become more than a trail, and was called the Wilderness Road. It was the safest way to Kentucky because the British and the Indians still had a hold on the Ohio River water route, the only other way to reach Kentucky.

Moving to Kentucky had been in Abraham Lincoln's

thoughts for some time, but he didn't finally decide to go until the state of Virginia started a land office and made new laws to help straighten out tangled land-titles in Kentucky.

While Bathsheba was still carrying in her arms the baby, Thomas, it happened that Abraham Lincoln sold his farm, and in accordance with the laws of Virginia she signed papers giving up her rights to her husband's land, declaring in writing on the 24th day of September, 1781, that "she freely and voluntarily relinquished the same without the Force threats or compulsion of her husband." Then they packed their belongings, especially the rifle, the ax, and the plow, and joined a party which headed down the Wilderness Road through Cumberland Gap and up north and west into Kentucky.

ABRAHAM AND BATHSHEBA (OR BATSAB) LINCOLN SIGN THEIR
NAMES TO A DEED IN THE COURTHOUSE OF ROCKINGHAM
COUNTY, VIRGINIA.

Tall mountains loomed about them with long blue shadows at sunup and sundown as they traveled, camped, broke

[7]

camp, and traveled again. And as they watched the mountains they slanted their keenest eyes on any moving patch of shrub or tree—the red men who ambushed enemies might be there.

There had been papers signed, and the land by law belonged to the white men, but the red men couldn't understand or didn't wish to understand how the land was gone from them to the white men. Besides, the red men had been fighting among themselves for favorite hunting grounds and fishing waters; there had been hundreds of years of fighting; now they were fighting white men by the same weapons, ways, and ambushes as they fought red men. And so, though the scenery was good to look at, the white men traveling the Wilderness Road kept a keen eye on the underbrush and had scouts ahead at the turn of the road and scouts behind.

Some towns and villages then were paying a dollar to two dollars apiece for Indian scalps.

Coming through safe to Kentucky, Abraham Lincoln located on the Green River, where he filed claims for more than two thousand acres. He had been there three or four years when, one day as he was working in a field, the rifle shot of an Indian killed him. His children and his children's children scattered across Kentucky, Tennessee, Indiana, and Illinois.

[8]

WILDERNESS ROAD TO KENTUCKY

Tom Lincoln, the child of Abraham and Bathsheba, while growing up, lived in different places in Kentucky, sometimes with his kith and kin, sometimes hiring out to

farmers, mostly in Washington County, and somehow be-tweenwhiles managing to learn the carpenter's trade and cabinet-making. He bought a horse—and paid taxes on it. He put in a year on the farm of his uncle, Isaac Lincoln,

[11]

on the Wautauga River in East Tennessee. He moved to Hardin County in Kentucky while still a young bachelor, and bought a farm on Mill Creek, paid taxes on the farm, kept out of debt, and once bought a pair of silk suspenders for a dollar and a half at a time when most men were using homemade hickory-bark galluses.

As Tom Lincoln came to his full growth he was about five feet, nine inches tall, weighing about 185 pounds, his muscles and ribs close-knit, so that one time a boy joking with him tried to find the places between his ribs but couldn't put a finger in between any place where a rib ended and the muscle began. His dark hazel eyes looked out from a round face, from under coarse black hair. He was a slow, careless man with quiet manners, would rather have people come and ask him to work on a job than to hunt the job himself. He liked to sit around and have his own thoughts.

He wasn't exactly lazy; he was sort of independent, and liked to be where he wasn't interfered with. A little slab of bacon with hoecake or a little corn-bread and milk every day, and he was satisfied. He drank whisky but not often. The sober Baptists saw more of him than those who were steady at licking up liquor. He was a wild buck at fighting, when men didn't let him alone. A man talked about a woman once in a way Tom Lincoln didn't like.

[12]

And in the fight that came, Tom bit a piece of the man's nose off. His neighbors knew him as a good man to let alone. And his neighbors knew him for a good workman, a handy man with the ax, the saw, the drawknife, and the hammer. Though he was short-spoken, he knew yarns, could crack jokes, and had a reputation as a story-teller when he got started. He never had much time for the alphabet, could read some, and could sign his name.

Church meetings interested him. He had been to cabins on Sunday mornings; the worshipers sat where it was half dark. Windows hadn't been cut in the walls; light came in through the door; words of the sermon came from a preacher in half-shadows. And he had gone to service in the evening when the cabin was lighted by the burning logs of the fireplace. Sometimes he felt stirred inside when a young woman kneeling on the floor would turn a passionate, longing face to the roof of the cabin and call, "Jesus, I give everything to thee. I give thee all. I give thee all. I am wholly thine!"

He had heard different preachers; some he liked better than others; some he was suspicious of; others he could listen to by the hour. There was a Reverend Jesse Head he had heard preach over at Springfield in Washington County, and he had a particular liking for Jesse Head, who was a good chair-maker, a good cabinet-maker, and an active exhorter in the branch of the Methodist church that stood against negro slavery and on that account had separated from the regular church. When Tom joined the Baptists it was in that branch of the church which was taking a stand against slavery.

CHAPTER II

DURING those years when Tom Lincoln was getting into his twenties, the country in Hardin County and around Elizabethtown was still wilderness, with only a few farms and settlements. Kentucky had been admitted to the Union of states; there were places in the state where civilization had dented the wilderness; but it was still a country of uncut timber, land unknown to the plow, a region where wolves and bear, wild animals and the Indians still claimed their rights and titles, with tooth and fang, claw and club and knife.

[15]

They talked in Elizabethtown about Miles Hart, who lived near by, and how he was killed by the Indians after he had used up his powder, how his wife Elizabeth and her two children were taken by the Indians, and how, on an outdoor march with the Indians, she was sent away, as Indian squaws were, by herself, to build a fire in the snow and give birth to her child. The child lived six months, but its mother was several years in the hands of the Indians before a Frenchman bought her near Detroit and sent her back to her relatives in Kentucky, where she again married and was raising a family. It was nearly twenty years since Elder John Gerrard, the Baptist preacher, had come to Hardin County. He preached nine months, and then one day, when a hunting party was surprised by Indians, all got away except Elder Gerrard, who was lame, and whether the Indians killed him, burned him at the stake, or took him along as a slave, nobody ever heard. There were many things to talk about around Elizabethtown. There was a negro living there called General Braddock, a free man; he had been given his freedom because, when his master's cabin was attacked by Indians, he had killed nine of the red men and saved the lives of his owner's family.

There was the time when Henry Helm and Dan Vertrees were killed by the Indians; a red man wrestled a gun away from a white man and had his war-ax raised to bring down and split the head of the white man; it was then Nicholas Miller, quick as a cat, made a jump, snatched the white man away and killed the Indian. One man who saw it, John Glenn, said, "Miller snatched the white man from the Indian as he would a chicken from a hawk." There was talk about how, even though the wilderness life was full of danger, men kept coming on, the Wilderness Road and the Ohio River bringing more and more settlers year by year, some speaking in one form or another the language of Daniel Boone, calling himself "an instrument ordained by God to settle the wilderness." Also there were those who knew that Dragging Canoe, chief of the Chicka-mauga tribe of Indians, after a powwow when white men and red signed papers at Wautauga, had pointed his finger northwest toward Kentucky, saying words translated as "Bloody ground! . . . And dark and difficult to settle." It seemed that the ground, the soil, and the lay of the land in Kentucky had an old name among the Indians as a land for war.

As the crossroads grew into settlements in Hardin County, there was hard feeling between the crowd around Elizabethtown and the settlers in the valley over near Hodgen's mill, about where the county seat should be located and the courthouse built. On election days, when the members of the county board were chosen, the voters clashed. The hard feeling lasted nearly ten years. At least fifty combats of fist and skull took place, though it was generally understood that the only time the fighting was not strictly fair and square rough-and-tumble combat was when a young man named Bruce tried to gash his enemies by kicking them with shoes pointed with sharp iron pieces shaped like the "gaffs" which are fastened to the feet of fighting cocks, Bruce himself being a rooster-fight sport.

The first jail in Elizabethtown cost the county $42.60. The sheriff was discouraged with it, and in 1797 a new jail was built, costing $700.00, with stocks and whipping-post. Many of the prisoners were in for debt and both white and black men were lashed on their naked backs at the public whipping-post. The stocks were built so that each prisoner had to kneel with his hands and head clamped between two grooved planks. If the prisoner was dead drunk he was laid on his back with his feet in the stocks and kept there till he was sober.

The same year the jail was built, it happened that a man in for debt set fire to it when the jailer was away; the prisoner was nearly roasted to death but was saved, though the jail burned down; after which he was indicted for arson, and acquitted because he was a first-rate bricklayer and the town needed his work.

COPPER FACES AND WHITE

The time of the grand "raisin'" of the courthouse in 1795 in the middle of August was remembered; on that day forty strong men raised the frames and big logs into place while many women and children looked on, and at noon the men all crowded into the Haycraft double log-house to eat hearty from loaves of bread baked in a clay oven, roast shotes, chickens, ducks, potatoes, roast beef with cabbage and beans, old-fashioned baked custard and pudding, pies, pickles, and "fixin's."

Grand juries held their sessions in the woods alongside the courthouse. In 1798 their entire report was, "We present Samuel Forrester for profane swearing"; on several occasions they mention Isaac Hynes, the sheriff, for "profane swearing." The sheriff was a distiller and his still-house was in one year recommended for use as the county jail.

When people spoke of "the time Jacob was hung," they meant the year 1796 and the negro slave, Jacob, who was "reproved for sloth" and killed his owner with an ax; a jury fixed the value of the slave at 80 pounds, or $400; he broke jail, was taken again, and on hanging day the sheriff hired another black man "to tie the noose and drive the cart from under," leaving the murderer hanging in mid-air from the scaffold. A large crowd came in Sunday clothes, with lunch baskets, to see the law take its course.

If in that country they wished to speak of lighter things, they could talk about pancakes; it was a saying that a smart woman, a cook who was clever, could toss a pancake off the skillet up through the top of the chimney and run out-doors and catch it coming down. Eggs were five cents a dozen. And one year a defendant in a case at law got a new trial on showing that in his case the jury, after retir-ing and before agreeing on a verdict, "did eat, drink, fid-dle, and dance." Such were some of the community human cross-weaves in the neighborhood where Tom Lincoln spent the years just before he married.

CHAPTER III

Tom Lincoln was looking for a woman to travel through life with, for better or worse. He visited at the place of Christopher Bush, a hard-working farmer who came from German parents and had raised a family of sons with muscle. "There was no back-out in them; they never shunned a fight when they considered it necessary; and nobody ever heard one of them cry 'Enough.'"

Also there were two daughters with muscle and with shining faces and steady eyes. Tom Lincoln passed by Hannah and gave his best jokes to Sarah Bush. But it happened

[23]

that Sarah Bush wanted Daniel Johnston for a husband and he wanted her.

Another young woman Tom's eyes fell on was a brunette sometimes called Nancy Hanks because she was a daughter of Lucy Hanks, and sometimes called Nancy Sparrow because she was an adopted daughter of Thomas and Elizabeth Sparrow and lived with the Sparrow family.

Lucy Hanks had welcomed her child Nancy into life in Virginia in 1784 and had traveled the Wilderness Road carrying what was to her a precious bundle through Cumberland Gap and on into Kentucky.

The mother of Nancy was nineteen years old when she made this trip, leaving Nancy's father back in Virginia. She could croon in the moist evening twilight to the shining face in the sweet bundle, "Hush thee, hush thee, thy father's a gentleman." She could toss the bundle into the air against a far, hazy line of blue mountains, catch it in her two hands as it came down, let it snuggle to her breast and feed, while she asked, "Here we come—where from?"

And while Nancy was still learning to walk and talk, her mother Lucy was talked about in and around Harrodsburg, Kentucky, as too free and easy in her behavior, too wild in her ways.

What was clear in the years that had passed was that

Lucy Hanks was strong and strange, loved love and loved babies, had married a man she wanted, Henry Sparrow, and nine children had come and they were all learning to read and write under her teaching. Since she had married the talk about her running wild had let down.

After she married Henry Sparrow her daughter Nancy went under the roof of Thomas Sparrow, a brother of Henry, and Elizabeth Hanks Sparrow, a sister of Lucy. Under the same roof was an adopted boy named Dennis Hanks, a son of a Nancy Hanks who was one of three sisters of Lucy. There were still other Nancy Hankses in Hardin County and those who spoke of any Nancy Hanks often had to mention which one they meant.

Tom Lincoln had seen this particular Nancy Hanks living with the Sparrows and noticed she was shrewd and dark and lonesome. He had heard her tremulous voice and seen her shaken with sacred desires in church camp-meetings; he had seen her at preachings in cabins when her face stood out as a sort of picture in black against the fire-lights of the burning logs. He knew she could read the Bible, and had read in other books. She had seen a few newspapers and picked out pieces of news and read her way through.

Her dark skin, dark brown hair, keen little gray eyes, outstanding forehead, somewhat accented chin and cheek-bones, body of slender build, weighing about 130 pounds —these formed the outward shape of a woman carrying something strange and cherished along her ways of life. She was sad with sorrows like dark stars in blue mist. The hope was burned deep in her that beyond the harsh clay paths, the everyday scrubbing, washing, patching, fixing, the babble and the gabble of today, there are pastures and purple valleys of song.

She had seen tall hills there in Kentucky. She had seen the stark backbone of Muldraugh's Hill become folded in thin evening blankets with a lavender mist sprayed by sunset lights, and for her there were the tongues of promises over it all.

She believed in God, in the Bible, in mankind, in the past and future, in babies, people, animals, flowers, fishes, in foundations and roofs, in time and the eternities outside of time; she was a believer, keeping in silence behind her gray eyes more beliefs than she spoke. She knew . . . so much of what she believed was yonder—always yonder. Every day came scrubbing, washing, patching, fixing. There was so little time to think or sing about the glory she believed in. It was always yonder. . . .

The day came when Thomas Lincoln signed a bond with his friend, Richard Berry, in the courthouse at Springfield in Washington County, over near where his brother,

THOMAS AND NANCY

Mordecai, was farming, and the bond gave notice: "There is a marriage shortly intended between Thomas Lincoln and Nancy Hanks." It was June 10, 1806. Two days later, at Richard Berry's place, Beechland, a man twenty-eight years old and a woman twenty-three years old came before the Reverend Jesse Head, who later gave the county clerk the names of Thomas Lincoln and Nancy Hanks as having been "joined together in the Holy Estate of Matrimony agreeable to the rules of the Methodist Episcopal Church."

After the wedding came "the infare," the Kentucky style wedding celebration. One who was there said, "We had bear-meat, venison, wild turkey and ducks, eggs wild and tame, maple sugar lumps tied on a string to bite off for coffee or whisky, syrup in big gourds, peach-and-honey; a sheep that two families barbecued whole over coals of wood burned in a pit, and covered with green boughs to keep the juices in; and a race for the whisky bottle."

The new husband put his June bride on his horse and they rode away on the red clay road along the timber trails to Elizabethtown. Their new home was in a cabin close to the courthouse. Tom worked at the carpenter's trade, made cabinets, door-frames, window sash, and coffins. A daughter was born and they named her Sarah. Tom's reputation as a solid, reliable man, whose word could be depended on, was improved after his quarrels with Denton Geoheagan.

He took a contract to cut timbers and help put up a new sawmill for Geoheagan; and when Geoheagan wouldn't pay he went to law and won the suit for his pay. Geoheagan then started two suits against Lincoln, claiming the sawmill timbers were not cut square and true. Lincoln beat him in both suits, and noticed that afterward people looked to him as a reliable man whose word could be depended on.

It was about this time the building of the third Hardin County jail was finished in Elizabethtown, with an old-time dungeon underground. The first jailer was Reverend Benjamin Ogden, who was a Methodist preacher, also a chair-maker and worker in wood.

In May and the blossom-time of the year 1808, Tom and Nancy with little Sarah moved out from Elizabethtown to the farm of George Brownfield, where Tom did carpenter work and helped farm.

The Lincolns had a cabin of their own to live in. It stood among wild crab-apple trees.

And the smell of wild crab-apple blossoms, and the low crying of all wild things, came keen that summer to the nostrils of Nancy Hanks.

The summer stars that year shook out pain and warning, strange laughters, for Nancy Hanks.

CHAPTER IV

THE same year saw the Lincolns moved to a place on the
Big South Fork of Nolin's Creek, about two and a half
miles from Hodgenville. They were trying to farm a little
piece of ground and make a home. The house they lived
in was a cabin of logs cut from the timber near by.

The floor was packed-down dirt. One door, swung on
leather hinges, let them in and out. One small window
gave a lookout on the weather, the rain or snow, sun and
trees, and the play of the rolling prairie and low hills. A
stick-clay chimney carried the fire smoke up and away.

One morning in February of this year, 1809, Tom Lincoln came out of his cabin to the road, stopped a neighbor and asked him to tell "the granny woman," Aunt Peggy Walters, that Nancy would need help soon.

On the morning of February 12, a Sunday, the granny woman was there at the cabin. And she and Tom Lincoln and the moaning Nancy Hanks welcomed into a world of battle and blood, of whispering dreams and wistful dust, a new child, a boy.

A little later that morning Tom Lincoln threw some extra wood on the fire, and an extra bearskin over the mother, went out of the cabin, and walked two miles up the road to where the Sparrows, Tom and Betsy, lived. Dennis Hanks, the nine-year-old boy adopted by the Sparrows, met Tom at the door.

In his slow way of talking—he was a slow and a quiet man—Tom Lincoln told them, "Nancy's got a boy baby." * * A half-sheepish look was in his eyes, as though maybe more babies were not wanted in Kentucky just then.

The boy, Dennis Hanks, took to his feet, down the road to the Lincoln cabin. There he saw Nancy Hanks on a bed of poles cleated to a corner of the cabin, under warm bearskins.

She turned her dark head from looking at the baby to

* * *These words are from the Eleanor Atkinson interview with Dennis Hanks. Throughout this work conversational utterances are based word for word on sources deemed authentic.—The Author.*

look at Dennis and threw him a tired, white smile from her mouth and gray eyes. He stood by the bed, his eyes wide open, watching the even, quiet breaths, of this fresh, soft red baby.

"What you goin' to name him, Nancy?" the boy asked.

"Abraham," was the answer, "after his grandfather."

Soon came Betsy Sparrow. She washed the baby, put a yellow petticoat and a linsey shirt on him, cooked dried berries with wild honey for Nancy, put the one-room cabin in better order, kissed Nancy and comforted her, and went home.

Little Dennis rolled up in a bearskin and slept by the fireplace that night. He listened for the crying of the newborn child once in the night and the feet of the father moving on the dirt floor to help the mother and the little one. In the morning he took a long look at the baby and said to himself, "Its skin looks just like red cherry pulp squeezed dry, in wrinkles."

He asked if he could hold the baby. Nancy, as she passed the little one into Dennis's arms, said, "Be keerful, Dennis, fur you air the fust boy he's ever seen."

And Dennis swung the baby back and forth, keeping up a chatter about how tickled he was to have a new cousin to play with. The baby screwed up the muscles of its face and began crying with no let-up.

[33]

Dennis turned to Betsy Sparrow, handed her the baby and said to her, "Aunt, take him! He'll never come to much."

So came the birth of Abraham Lincoln that 12th of February in the year 1809—in silence and pain from a wilderness mother on a bed of corn-husks and bearskins—with an early laughing child prophecy he would never come to much.

And though he was born in a house with only one door and one window, it was written he would come to know many doors, many windows; he would read many riddles and doors and windows.

The Lincoln family lived three crop years on the farm where baby Abraham was born. It was a discouraging piece of land with yellow and red clay, stony soils, thick under-brush, land known as "barrens." It was called the Rock Spring farm because at the foot of one of its sloping hills the rocks curved in like the beginning of a cave; coats of moss spotted the rocks and rambled with quiet streaks of green over the gray; a ledge of rock formed a beckoning roof with room for people to stand under; and at the heart of it, for its center, was a never-ending flow of clear, cool water.

With the baby she called Abe in her arms, Nancy Hanks came to this Rock Spring more than once, sitting with her

"HE'LL NEVER COME TO MUCH!"

child and her thoughts, looking at running water and green moss. The secrets of the mingled drone and hush of the place gave her reminders of Bible language, "Be ye comforted," or "Peace, be still."

Cooking, washing, sewing, spinning, weaving, helping

keep a home for a man and two babies, besides herself, in a one-room cabin, took a good deal of her time. If there were flies creeping over the face of the baby Abe, she had to drop her work and shoo the flies away. There were few hours in the year she was free to sit with her child and her thoughts, listening to the changing drone and hush of Rock Spring saying, "Be ye comforted," or "Peace, be still."

The baby grew, learning to sit up, to crawl over the dirt floor of the cabin; the gristle became bone; the father joked about the long legs getting longer; the mother joked about how quick he grew out of one shirt into another.

Sparrows and Hankses who came visiting said, "He's solemn as a papoose." An easy and a light bundle he was to carry when the family moved to a farm on Knob Creek, eight miles from Hodgenville, on the main highway from Louisville to Nashville.

CHAPTER V

On the Knob Creek farm the child Abraham Lincoln learned to talk, to form words with the tongue and the roof of the mouth and the force of the breath from lungs and throat. "Pappy" and "Mammy," the words of his people meaning father and mother, were among the first syllables. He learned what the word "name" meant; his name was Abraham, the same as Abraham in the Bible, the same as his grandfather Abraham. It was "Abe" for short; if his mother called in the dark, "Is that you, Abe?" he answered, "Yes, Mammy, it's me." The name of the family he belonged to was "Lincoln" or "Linkun," though most people called it "Linkern" and it was sometimes spelled "Linkhorn."

The family lived there on Knob Creek farm, from the time Abe was three or so till he was past seven years of age. Here he was told "Kaintucky" meant the state he was living in; Knob Creek farm, the Rock Spring farm where he was born, Hodgenville, Elizabethtown, Muldraugh's Hill, these places he knew, the land he walked on, was all part of Kentucky.

Yet it was also part of something bigger. Men had been fighting, bleeding, and dying in war, for a country, "our country"; a man couldn't have more than one country any more than he could have more than one mother; the name of the mother country was the "United States"; and there was a piece of cloth with red and white stripes having a blue square in its corner filled with white stars; and this piece of cloth they called "a flag." The flag meant the "United States." One summer morning his father started the day by stepping out of the front door and shooting a long rifle into the sky; and his father explained it was the day to make a big noise because it was the "Fourth of July," the day the United States first called itself a "free and independent" nation.

His folks talked like other folks in the neighborhood. They called themselves "pore" people. A man learned in books was "eddicated." What was certain was "sartin." The syllables came through the nose; joints were "j'ints"; fruit "spiled" instead of spoiling; in corn-planting time they "drapped" the seeds. They went on errands and "brung" things back. Their dogs "follered" the coons.

Flannel was "flannen," a bandanna a "bandanner," a chimney a "chimbly," a shadow a "shadder," and mosquitoes plain "skeeters." They "gethered" crops. A creek was a "crick," a cover a "kiver."

A man silent was a "say-nothin'." They asked, "Have ye et?" There were dialogues, "Kin ye?" "No, I cain't." And if a woman had an idea of doing something she said, "I had a idy to." They made their own words. Those who spoke otherwise didn't belong, were "puttin' on." This was their wilderness lingo; it had gnarled bones and gaunt hours of their lives in it.

Words like "independent" bothered the boy. He was hungry to understand the meanings of words. He would ask what "independent" meant and when he was told the meaning he lay awake nights thinking about the meaning of the meaning of "independent." Other words bothered him, such as "predestination." He asked the meaning of that and lay awake hours at night thinking about the meaning of the meaning.

CHAPTER VI

Seven-year-old Abe walked four miles a day going to the Knob Creek school to learn to read and write. Zachariah Riney and Caleb Hazel were the teachers who brought him along from A B C to where he would write the name "A-b-r-a-h-a-m L-i-n-c-o-l-n" and count numbers beginning with one, two, three, and so on. He heard twice two is four.

The schoolhouse was built of logs, with a dirt floor, no window, one door. The scholars learned their lessons by saying them to themselves out loud till it was time to recite; alphabets, multiplication tables, and the letters of spelled words were all in the air at once. It was a "blab school"; so they called it.

The Louisville and Nashville pike running past the Lincoln cabin had many different travelers. Covered wagons came with settlers moving south and west, or north to Ohio and Indiana; there were peddlers with knickknacks to spread out and tell the prices of; congressmen, members of the legislature meeting at Lexington, men who had visited Henry Clay at Ashland.

Coming back from a fishing trip, with one fish, Abe met a soldier who came from fighting in the Battle of New Orleans with General Jackson, and Abe, remembering his father and mother had told him to be good to soldiers, handed the soldier the one fish.

The Lincolns got well acquainted with Christopher Columbus Graham, a doctor, a scientist, who was beginning to study and write books about the rocks, flowers, plants, trees, and wild animals of Kentucky; Graham slept in the bed while the Lincolns slept on the floor of the cabin, more than once; he told in the evening talk about days camping with Daniel Boone, and running backward with Boone so as to make foot-tracks pointing forward to mislead the Indians; he talked about stones, leaves, bones, snake-skins he was carrying in a sack back to Louisville;

he mentioned a young storekeeper at Elizabethtown, named John James Audubon, who had marvelous ways with birds and might some day write a great book about birds. The boy Abe heard traveling preachers and his father talk about the times when they held church meetings in cabins, and every man had his rifle by his side, and there were other men with rifles outside the cabin door, ready for Indians who might try to interrupt their Sabbath worship. And the boy never liked it when the talkers slung around words like "independent" and "predestination," because he lay awake thinking about those long words.

Abe was the chore-boy of the Knob Creek farm as soon as he grew big enough to run errands, to hold a pine-knot at night lighting his father at a job, or to carry water, fill the woodbox, clean ashes from the fireplace, hoe weeds, pick berries, grapes, persimmons for beer-making. He hunted the timbers and came back with walnuts, hickory and hazel nuts. His hands knew the stinging blisters from using a hoe-handle back and forth a summer afternoon, and in autumn the mash of walnut-stain that wouldn't wash off, with all the rinsing and scrubbing of Nancy Hanks's homemade soap. He went swimming with Austin Gollaher; they got their backs sunburnt so the skin peeled off.

Wearing only a shirt—no hat nor pants—Abe rode a horse hitched to a "bull-tongue" plow of wood shod with iron. He helped his father with seed corn, beans, onions, potatoes. He ducked out of the way of the heels of the

stallion and brood mares his father kept and paid taxes on.

The father would ride away to auctions, once coming home with dishes, plates, spoons, and a wash basin, another time with a heifer, and again with a wagon that had been knocked down to the highest bidder for 8½ cents.

Abe and his sister picked pails of currants and blueberries for mother Nancy to spread in the sun to dry and put away for winter eating. There were wild grapes and pawpaws; there were bee trees with wild honey; there were wild crab-apples and red haws. If it was a good corn year, the children helped shell the corn by hand and put it between two big flat stones, grinding it into cornmeal. The creeks gave them fish to fry. Tom Lincoln took his gun and brought back prairie turkey, partridge, rabbit, sometimes a coon, a bear, or a deer; and the skins of these big animals were tanned, cut and sewed into shirts, trousers, moccasins; the coonskins made caps.

There were lean times and fat, all depending on the weather, the rains or floods, how Tom Lincoln worked and what luck he had fishing and hunting. There were times when they lived on the fat of the land and said God was good; other times when they just scraped along and said they hoped the next world would be better than this one.

It was wilderness. Life dripped with fat and ease. Or it took hold with hunger and cold. All the older settlers remembered winter in the year 1795, when "cold Friday" came; Kentucky was "cold as Canada," and cows froze to death in the open fields. The wilderness is careless.

Between the roadway over the top of Muldraugh's Hill and the swimming-hole where Abe Lincoln and Austin Gollaher ducked each other, there are tall hills more correctly called limestone bluffs. They crowd around Knob Creek and shape the valley's form. Their foundations are

[46]

WILDERNESS LUCK

rocks, their measurements seem to be those of low mountains rather than hills. They seem to be aware of proportions and to suggest a quiet importance and secrets of fire, erosion, water, time, and many repeated processes that have stood them against the sky so that human settlers in the valley feel that around them are speakers of reserves and immensities.

The valley through which Knob Creek wanders there near Muldraugh's Hill, shooting its deep rushes of water when the hill rains flush the bottoms, has many keepers of the darker reticences of the crust of the earth and the changers that hold on to their lives there. That basic stream has a journal of its movement among pools inconceivably quiet in their mirrorings during days when the weather is fair and the elements of the sky at ease, and again of movement among those same pools when the rampages between the limestone banks send the water boiling and swirling. The naming of Muldraugh's Hill was a rich act in connotation, for it has whisperings of namelessly shrewd and beautiful wishes that the older and darker landscapes of Ireland breathe.

Trees crowd up its slopes with passionate footholds as though called by homes in the rocky soil; their climbings have covered sides and crests till they murmur, "You shall see no tall hills here unless you look at us." Caverns and ledges thrust their surprises of witchery and wizardry, of gnomes and passwords, or again of old-time intimations and analogues, memories of reckless rains leaving wave-prints to hint or say Muldraugh's Hill and the Knob Creek valley are old-timers in the making of the world, old-timers alongside of the two-footed little mover known as man. In the bottom lands the honeysuckle ranges with a strength nothing less than fierce; so deep are its roots that, unless torn away by the machines of man, the bees count on every year a boomer harvest of its honey-stuff; black and brown butterflies, spotted and streaked with scrolls and alphabets of unknown tongues from the world of wings— these come back every year to the honeysuckle.

Redbud, wild rose, and white daisies that look like scatterings of snow on green levels rise up with their faces yearly. Birds have made the valley a home; oncoming civilization has not shut off their hopes; homes for all are here; the martins learned a thousand years before the white man came that ten martins that fight with despair can kill and pick the eyes out of the head of a hawk that comes to slaughter and eat martins. And horses have so loved the valley, and it has so loved them in return, that some of the fastest saddle and riding nags remembered of men got their flying starts here.

Such was the exterior of the place and neighborhood

where Abe Lincoln grew up from three to seven years of age, where he heard travelers talk, where he learned to write and sign his name, where, in fact, he first learned the meanings of names and how to answer, "Yes, it's me," if his mother called in the dark, "Is that you, Abe?"

CHAPTER VII

In the year 1816 Tom Lincoln was appointed road surveyor. The paper naming him for that office said he was
named in place of George Redman to repair the road
"leading from Nolen to Pendleton, which lies between the
Bigg Hill and the Rolling Fork." It further commanded
"that all hands that assisted said Redman do assist Lincoln
in keeping said road in repair." It was a pasty red clay
road. That the county was beginning to think about good
roads showed that civilization was breaking through on
the wilderness. And that Tom Lincoln was named as road
surveyor showed they were holding some respect for him
as a citizen and taxpayer of that community. At the county
courthouse the recorder of deeds noticed that Thomas Lin-

coln signed his name, while his wife, Nancy, made her mark.

Thomas Lincoln

Nancy L. Lincoln
her mark

Knob Creek settlers taking their corn to Hodgens Mill or riding to Elizabethtown to pay their taxes at the court or collect bounties on wolfskins at the county courthouse, talked a good deal about land-titles, landowners, landlords, land-laws, land-lawyers, land-sharks. Tom Lincoln about that time was chopping down trees and cutting brush on the Knob Creek land so as to clear more ground, raise corn on it and make a farm out of it. And he wasn't satisfied; he was suspicious that even if he did get his thirty acres cleared and paid for, the land might be taken away from him. This was happening to other settlers; they had the wrong kind of papers. Pioneers and settlers who for years had been fighting Indians, wolves, foxes, mosquitoes, and malaria had seen their land taken away; they had the wrong kind of papers. Daniel Boone, the first man to break a path from civilization through and into the Kentucky wilderness, found himself one day with all his rich, blue-grass Kentucky lands gone, not an acre of his big farms left; he had the wrong kind of papers; that was why he moved from Kentucky to Missouri.

[53]

Though Tom Lincoln was paying taxes on his thirty-acre farm, he was sued as a "tresspasser." He had to prove he wasn't a squatter—which he did. He went to court and won his suit. His little thirty-acre piece was only one of many pieces of a 10,000-acre tract surveyed in 1784 and patented to one man, Thomas Middleton, in 1786.

Poor white men were having a harder time to get along. Hardin County had been filling up with negroes, slave black men, bought and sold among the rich and well-to-do. The Hodgens, La Rues, and other first families usually had one or two, or six or a dozen, negroes. More than half the population of Hardin County were colored. And it seemed that as more slave black men were brought in, a poor white man didn't count for so much; he had a harder time to get along; he was free with the freedom of him who cannot be sold nor bought, while the black slave was free with the security of the useful horse, mule, cow, goat, or dog whose life and health is worth money to the owner.

Already, in parts of Kentucky and farther south, the poor white men, their women and children, were using the name of "nigger" for the slaves, while there were black slaves in families of quality who used the name of "po' w'ite" for the white people who owned only their clothes, furniture, a rifle, an ax, perhaps a horse and plow, and no land, no slaves, no stables, and no property to speak of.

[54]

DANIEL BOONE

While these changes were coming in Kentucky, the territory of Indiana came into the Union as a state whose law declared "all men are born equally free and independent" and "the holding any part of the human creation in slavery, or involuntary servitude, can only originate in usurpation and tyranny." In crossing the Ohio River's two shores, a traveler touched two soils, one where the buying and selling of black slaves went on, the other where the negro was held to be "part of human creation" and was not property for buying and selling. But both soils were part of the Union of states.

Letters and reports reaching Hardin County about this time told of rich, black lands in Indiana, with more bushels of corn to the acre than down in Kentucky, Government land with clear title, the right kind of papers, for two dollars an acre. This helped Tom Lincoln to decide in the year 1816 to move to Indiana. He told the family he would build a flatboat, load the household goods on it, float by creeks to the Ohio River, leave the household goods somewhere along the river while he went afoot up into Indiana, located his land, and registered it. Then he would come back, and the family, afoot and on horseback, would move to the new farm and home.

CHAPTER VIII

THE boy, Abe, had his thoughts, some running ahead wondering how Indiana would look, some going back to his seven little years in Kentucky. Here he had curled around his mother's apron, watched her face and listened to her reading the Bible at the cabin log-fire, her fingers rambling through his hair, the hands patting him on the cheek and under the chin. God was real to his mother; he tried to make pictures in his head of the face of God far off and away in the sky, watching Kentucky, Hodgenville, Knob Creek, and all the rest of the world He had made. His thoughts could go back to the first time on a winter night around the fire when he lay flat on his stomach listening to his father as he told about his brothers, Mordecai and Josiah, and their father, Abraham Lincoln, who had staked out claims for more than 2,000 acres of land on the Green River. One day Abraham Lincoln and his three boys were working in a field; all of a sudden the father doubled up with a groan of pain and crumpled to the ground, just after the boys had heard a rifle-shot and the whining of a bullet. "Indians," the boys yelled to each other.

And Mordecai ran to a cabin, Josiah started across the fields and woods to a fort to bring help, while Tom Lincoln—little knee-high Tom—stooped over his father's bleeding body and wondered what he could do. He looked up to see an Indian standing over him, and a shining bangle hanging down over the Indian's shoulder close to the heart.

The Indian clutched upward with his hands, doubled with a groan and crumpled to the ground; Mordecai with a rifle at a peephole in the cabin had aimed his rifle at the shining bangle hanging down close to the Indian's heart, and Tom was so near he heard the bullet plug its hole into the red man.

And for years after that Mordecai Lincoln hated Indians with a deadly hate; if he heard that Indians were loose anywhere in a half-day's riding, he took his best rifles, pistols, and knives, and went Indian-killing.

There was Dr. Christopher Columbus Graham from

Louisville, telling how the Indians were chasing Daniel Boone, and Boone saw a grapevine climbing high up a big oak; and he cut the grapevine near the root, took a run and a swing and made a jump of forty feet, so the Indians had to lose time finding sight and smell of his foot-tracks again.

And there were caves, worth remembering about in that part of Kentucky, and especially the biggest one of all, Mammoth Cave, fifty miles south; they said a thousand wagons could drive in and there would be room for another thousand.

And there was the foxy Austin Gollaher, his playmate. Up a tree he climbed one time, Abe dropped a pawpaw down into a coonskin cap; he guessed it was Austin's cap he was putting a smear of pawpaw mash in, but Austin had seen the trick coming and changed caps. So he had to wipe the smear out of his own cap.

Once he was walking on a log across Knob Creek when the rains had raised the creek. Just under the log, and under his feet, was the rush of the yellow muddy water. The log was slippery, his feet slippery. His feet went up in the air, he tumbled to the bottom of the creek; he came up, slipped again, came up with his nose and eyes full of water, and then saw Austin Gollaher on the bank holding out a long pole. He took hold of the pole and Austin pulled him to the bank.

Maybe he would grow up; his feet would be farther away from his head and his chin if he grew up; he could pick apples without climbing a tree or throwing clubs—

if he grew up. Maybe then, after growing up, he would know more about those words he heard men saying, "in-de-pend-ent," "pre-des-ti-na-tion." Daniel Boone—yes, he could understand about Daniel Boone—wearing moccasins and a buckskin shirt. But George Washington and

Thomas Jefferson, and the President in Washington, James Madison—they were far off; they were sort of like God; it was hard to make pictures of their faces.

How many times he had gone to the family Bible, opened the big front cover, and peeped in at the page which tells what the book is! There were the words: "The Holy Bible, containing the Old and New Testaments, with Arguments prefixed to the Different Books and Moral and Theological Observations illustrating each Chapter, composed by the Reverend Mr. Osterwald, Professor of Divinity." And then pages and pages filled with words spelled out like the words in the spelling-book he had in school. So many words: heavy words—mysterious words!

About wolf heads, he could understand. He saw a man in Elizabethtown one time carrying two big wolf heads. The man had shot the wolves and was going to the courthouse, where they paid money for wolf heads. Yes, this he could understand. Wolves kill sheep and cattle in the fields; they come to the barns for pigs and chickens; he had heard them howling and sniffing on winter nights around the Knob Creek cabin and up the hills and gorges.

And there was his mother, his "mammy," the woman other people called Nancy or Nancy Hanks. . . . It was so dark and strange about her. There was such sweetness. Yet there used to be more sweetness and a fresher sweet-

[62]

ness. There had been one baby they buried. Then there was Sally—and him, little Abe. Did the children cost her something? Did they pull her down? . . . The baby that came and was laid away so soon, only three days after it

came, in so little a grave: that hurt his mother; she was sick and tired more often after that. . . . There were such lights and shadows back in her eyes. She wanted—what did she want? There were more and more days he had to take care of her, when he loved to bring cool drinking water to her—or anything she asked for.

Well—a boy seven years old isn't supposed to know much; he goes along and tries to do what the big people tell him to do. . . . They have been young and seen trouble: maybe they know. . . . He would get up in the morning when they called him; he would run to the spring for water. . . . He was only seven years old—and there were lots of frisky tricks he wanted to know more about.

He was a "shirt-tail boy." . . . Three boys teased him one day when he took corn to Hodgen's Mill; they wouldn't be satisfied till he had punched their noses. . . . A clerk in the store at Elizabethtown gave him maple sugar to sit on a syrup keg and suck while his mother bought salt and flour. And the clerk was the only man he knew who was wearing store clothes, Sunday clothes, every day in the week. . . . The two pear trees his father planted on the Rock Spring farm . . . the faces of two goats a man kept down in Hodgenville . . . Dennis Hanks saying, "Abe, your face is solemn as a papoose."

It wouldn't be easy to forget that Saturday afternoon in corn-planting time when other boys dropped the seed-corn into all the rows in the big seven-acre field—and Abe dropped the pumpkin seed. He dropped two seeds at every other hill and every other row. The next Sunday morning there came a big rain in the hills; it didn't rain a drop in the valley, but the water came down the gorges and slides, and washed ground, corn, pumpkin seeds, and all clear off the field.

A dark blur of thoughts, pictures, memories and hopes moved through the head of little seven-year-old Abe. The family was going to move again. There was hope of better luck up north in Indiana. Tom's older brother, Josiah, was farming along the Big Blue River. Rich black corn-land was over there in "Indianny," more bushels to the acre than anywhere in Kentucky.

CHAPTER IX

In the fall of the year 1816, Abe watched his father cut
down trees, cut out logs, and fasten those logs into a flatboat on Knob Creek. Abe ran after tools his father called
for, sometimes held a hammer, a saw and a knife in his
hands ready to give his father the next one called for. If
his father said, "Fetch me a drink of water," the boy
fetched; his legs belonged to his father. He helped carry
chairs, tables, household goods, and carpenter's tools, load-
ing them onto the flatboat. These, with four hundred gal-
lons of whisky, "ten bar'ls," Tom had loaded onto the
boat, made quite a cargo. Tom Lincoln, who was not much
of a drinking man, had traded his farm for whisky, which
was a kind of money in that day, and $20.00 cash.

Nancy Hanks and Sarah and Abe stayed on the farm
while the husband and father floated down Knob Creek to
Salt River and into the Ohio River. Tom was out of luck
when the flatboat turned over so that the tool chest, household goods and four barrels of whisky slid out of the boat.

Most of the whisky and some of the other goods he managed to fish up from the river bottom. Then he crossed the Ohio River, landed on the Indiana side at Thompson's Ferry and left his whisky and household goods at the house of a man called Posey.

He started off on foot into the big timbers of what was then Perry County, later divided into Spencer County. He decided to live and to farm on a quarter-section of land on Little Pigeon Creek; he notched the trees with his ax, cleared away brush and piled it, as the Government land-laws required. This was his "claim," later filed at the Land Office in Vincennes, Indiana, as the Southwest Quarter of Section Thirty-two, Town Four South, Range Five West, to be paid for at $2.00 an acre. His Indiana homestead was now ready for a cabin and a family; he walked back to the Knob Creek home in Kentucky and told the family he reckoned they'd all put in the winter up in "Indianny."

They had fifty miles to go, in a straight line "as the crow flies," but about one hundred miles with all the zig-zags and curves around hills, timbers, creeks, and rivers.

Pots, pans, kettles, blankets, the family Bible, and other things were put into bags and loaded on two horses. Nancy and Sarah climbed on one horse, Tom and Abe on the other. When it was hard going for the horses, the father and mother walked. Part of the way on that hundred-mile ride made little Abe's eyes open. They were going deeper into the wilderness. In Kentucky there were ten people to the square mile and in Indiana only three. As Abe sat on the horse plodding along, he saw miles and miles of beeches, oaks, elms, hard and soft maples, hung and run over with the scarlet streamers and the shifting gray hazes of autumn.

Then they came to the Ohio River. The Frenchmen years before named it "La Belle Rivière," meaning it was a sheen of water as good to look at as a beautiful woman. There she lay—the biggest stretch of shining water his eyes had ever seen. And Abe thought how different it was from Knob Creek, which he could walk across on a log— if he didn't let his feet slip from under. They crossed the river, and at the house of the man called Posey they got a wagon, loaded the barrels of whisky and the household goods, and drove sixteen miles to their "claim." The trail was so narrow that a few times Tom Lincoln got off the wagon with an ax and cut brush and trees so the wagon could pass through. It was a hired wagon and horses they came with, and the wagon and horse-team were taken back to Posey.

Tom Lincoln, his wife, boy, and girl, had arrived on a claim at Little Pigeon Creek, without a horse or a cow, without a house, with a little piece of land under their feet and the wintry sky high over. Naked they had come into the world; almost naked they came to Little Pigeon Creek, Indiana.

The whole family pitched in and built a pole-shed or "half-faced camp." On a slope of ground stood two trees about fourteen feet apart, east and west. These formed the two strong corner-posts of a sort of cabin with three sides, the fourth side open, facing south. The sides and the roof were covered with poles, branches, brush, dried grass, mud; chinks were stuffed where the wind or the rain was trying to come through. At the open side a log-fire was kept burning night and day. In the two far corners inside the camp were beds of dry leaves on the ground. To these beds the sleepers brought their blankets and bearskins.

Here they lived a year. In the summer time and fair weather, the pole-shed was snug enough. When the rain storms or wind and snow broke through and drenched the place, or when the south or southwest wind blew the fire-smoke into the camp so those inside had to clear out, it was a rough life.

The mother sang. Nancy Hanks knew songs her mother, Lucy, had heard in Virginia. The ballad of Fair Ellender told of the hero coming home with the Brown Girl who had lands and gold. Fair Ellender taunted: "Is this your bride? She seemeth me plagued brown." And for that, the

Brown Girl leaped over a table corner and put a slim little knife through Fair Ellender's heart. Then out came the hero's sword and he cut off the Brown Girl's head and

"slung it agin the wall." Then he put the sword through his own heart.

And there was the ballad of Wicked Polly, who danced and ran wild and told the old folks, "I'll turn to God when I get old, and He will then receive my soul." But when death struck her down while she was young and running wild, she called for her mother, and with rolling eyeballs,

[70]

cried, "When I am dead, remember well, your wicked Polly screams in hell."

Tom chopped logs for a cabin forty yards away while Abe did the best he could helping Nancy and Sarah trim the branches off the logs, cut brush, clear ground for planting, hoe weeds, tend the log-fire. The heaviest regular chore of the children was walking a mile away to a spring and carrying a bucket of water back home. Their food was mostly game shot in the woods near by; they went barefoot most of the year; in the winter their shoes were homemade moccasins; they were up with the sun and the early birds in the morning; their lighting at night was fire-logs and pine-knots. In summer and early fall the flies and mosquitoes swarmed.

In the new cabin Tom Lincoln was building, and on this Little Pigeon Creek farm, the Lincoln family was going to live fourteen years.

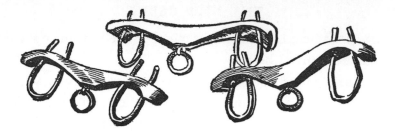

CHAPTER X

As Abe Lincoln, seven years old, going on eight, went to sleep on his bed of dry leaves in a corner of the pole-shed there on Little Pigeon Creek, in Indiana, in the winter of 1816, he had his thoughts, his feelings, his impressions. He shut his eyes, and looking-glasses began to work inside his head; he could see Kentucky and the Knob Creek farm again; he could see the Ohio River shining so far across that he couldn't begin to throw a stone from one side to the other.

And while his eyes were shut he could see the inside of the pole-shed, the floor of earth and grass, the frying-pan, the cooking-pot, the water-pail he and his sister carried full of water from the spring a mile away, and the log-fire always kept burning. And sometimes his imagination, his shut eyes and their quick-changing looking-glasses would bring the whole outdoor sky and land indoors, into the pole-shed, into the big shifting looking-glasses inside of his

head. The mystery of imagination, of the faculty of recon-
struction and piecing together today the things his eyes had
seen yesterday, this took hold of him and he brooded over
it.

One night he tried to sleep while his head was working
on the meaning of the heavy and mysterious words standing dark on the pages of the family Bible; the stories his
mother told him from those pages; all the people in the
world drowned, the world covered with water, even Indiana and Kentucky, all people drowned except Noah and
his family; the man Jonah swallowed by a whale and after
days coming out of the belly of the whale; the Last Day
to come, the stars dropping out of the sky, the world swallowed up in fire.

And one night this boy felt the southwest wind blowing
the log-fire smoke into his nostrils. And there was a hoot-
owl crying, and a shaking of branches in the beeches and
walnuts outside, so that he went to the south opening of
the shed and looked out on a winter sky with a high quarter-moon and a white shine of thin frost on the long open
spaces of the sky.

And an old wonder took a deeper hold on him, a wonder
about the loneliness of life down there in the Indiana wilderness, and a wonder about what was happening in other
places over the world, places he had heard people mention,

cities, rivers, flags, wars, Jerusalem, Washington, Baltimore.

He might have asked the moon, "What do you see?" And the moon might have told him many things.

That year of 1816 the moon had seen sixteen thousand wagons come along one turnpike in Pennsylvania, heading west, with people hungry for new land, a new home, just like Tom Lincoln. Up the Mississippi River that year had come the first steamboat to curve into the Ohio River and land passengers at Louisville. The moon had seen the first steamboat leave Pittsburgh and tie up at New Orleans. New wheels, wagons, were coming, an iron horse snorting fire and smoke. Rolling-mills, ingots, iron, steel, were the talk of Pennsylvania; a sheet copper mill was starting in Massachusetts.

The moon could see eight million people in the United States, white men who had pushed the Indians over the eastern mountains, fighting to clear the Great Plains and the southern valleys of the red men. At Fallen Timbers and at Tippecanoe in Indiana, and down at the Great Bend of the Tallapoosa, the pale faces and copper faces had yelled and grappled and Weatherford had said, "I have done the white people all the harm I could; if I had an army I would fight to the last; my warriors can no longer hear my voice; their bones are at Talladega, Tallushatches, Emuckfaw, and Tohopeka; I can do no more than weep." The red men had been warned by Jefferson to settle down and be farmers, to double their numbers every twenty years as the white people did, the whites in "new swarms continually advancing upon the country like flocks of pigeons."

The moon had seen two men, sunburned, wind-bitten and scarred, arrive at the White House just four years before Abe Lincoln was born. The two men had been on a three-year trip, leaving Washington in 1802, riding and walking across the Great Plains, the Rockies and Sierras, to the Pacific Coast country, and then back to Washington. What those two, Lewis and Clark, had to tell, opened the eyes of white people to what a rich, big country they lived in. Out along that trail Jefferson could see "new swarms advancing like flocks of pigeons."

And how had these eight million people come to America, for the moon to look down on and watch their westward swarming? Many were children of men who had quarreled in the old countries of Europe, and fought wars about the words and ways of worshiping God and obeying His commandments. They were Puritans from England, French Huguenots, German Pietists, Hanoverians, Moravians, Saxons, Austrians, Swiss, Quakers, all carrying their Bibles. Also there were Ulster Presbyterians from North Ireland, and Scotch Presbyterians. They came by their own wish. Others who came not by their own wish were fifty thousand thieves and murderers sent from British prisons and courts. Dr. Samuel Johnson, the same man who said, "Patriotism is the last refuge of a scoundrel," had called Americans "a race of convicts." Convicted men in England, offered the choice of hanging or being shipped to America, had given the answer, "Hang me."

The moon had seen boys and girls by thousands kidnaped off the streets of English cities and smuggled across to America. And each year for fifty years there had come a thousand to fifteen hundred "indentured servants," men and women who had signed papers to work for a certain master, the law holding them to work till their time was up.

The moon had seen sailing-ships start from ports in Europe and take from six weeks to six months crossing the Atlantic. Aboard those ships often were "stench, fumes, vomiting, many kinds of sicknesses, fever, dysentery, scurvey, the mouth-rot, and the like, all of which come from old and sharply salted food and meat, also from bad and foul water."

Such were a few of the things known to the fathers and grandfathers of part of the eight million people in Amer-

WHAT THE MOON SAW

ica that the moon was looking down on in the winter nights of 1816. And in the years to come the moon would see more and more people coming from Europe.

Seldom had the moon in its thousands of years of looking down on the earth and the human family seen such a man as the Napoleon Bonaparte whose bayonets had been going in Europe for fifteen years, shoving kings off thrones, changing laws, maps, books, raising armies, using them up, and raising new armies, until people in some regions were saying, "The red roses of this year grow from the blood-wet ground of the wars we fought last year." And at last the terrible Napoleon was caged, jailed, on the lonely island of St. Helena. Crying for the "liberty and equality" of France to be spread over the world, he had led armies to believe and dream of beating down all other armies in Europe that tried to stand against him. Then he was a lean shadow; he had become fat; the paunch stuck out farther than is allowed to conquerors. He had hugged armfuls of battle-flags to his breast while telling an army of soldiers, "I cannot embrace you all, but I do so in the person of your general." It hurt his ears when, captured and being driven in an open carriage, he heard sarcastic people along the streets mock at him with the call, "Long live the Emperor!" He would die far from home, with regrets, the first man to be Napoleonic.

When Napoleon sold to Jefferson the Great Plains between the Mississippi River and the Rocky Mountains, the moon saw only a few Indians, buffalo hunters and drifters, living there. The price for the land was fifteen million dollars; Jefferson had to argue with people who said the price was too high. Such things the moon had seen. Also, out of war-taxed and war-crippled Europe the moon could see steady lines of ships taking people from that part of the Round World across the water to America. Also, lines of ships sailing to Africa with whisky, calico, and silk, and coming back loaded with negroes.

And as the wagons, by thousands a year, were slipping through the passes of the Allegheny Mountains, heading west for the two-dollar-an-acre Government land, many steered clear of the South; they couldn't buy slaves; and they were suspicious of slavery; it was safer to go farming where white men did all the work. At first the stream of wagons and settlers moving west had kept close to the Ohio River. Then it began spreading in a fan-shape up north and west.

The moon could see along the pikes, roads, and trails heading west, broken wagon-wheels with prairie grass growing up over the spokes and hubs. And near by, sometimes, a rusty skillet, empty moccasins, and the bones of horses and men.

In the hot dog-days, in the long rains, in the casual blizzards, they had stuck it out—and lost. There came a saying, a pithy, perhaps brutal folk proverb, "The cowards never started and the weak ones died by the way."

Such were a few of the many, many things the moon might have told little Abe Lincoln, nearly eight years old, on a winter night in 1816 on Little Pigeon Creek, in the Buckhorn Valley, in southern Indiana—a high quarter-moon with a white shine of thin frost on the long open spaces of the sky.

He was of the blood and breath of many of these things, and would know them better in the years to come.

CHAPTER XI

DURING the year 1817, little Abe Lincoln, eight years old, going on nine, had an ax put in his hands and helped his father cut down trees and notch logs for the corners of their new cabin, forty yards from the pole-shed where the family was cooking, eating, and sleeping.

Wild turkey, ruffed grouse, partridge, coon, rabbit, were to be had for the shooting of them. Before each shot Tom Lincoln took a rifle-ball out of a bag and held the ball in his left hand; then with his right hand holding the gun-powder horn he pulled the stopper with his teeth, slipped the powder into the barrel, followed with the ball; then he rammed the charge down the barrel with a hickory ramrod held in both hands, looked to his trigger, flint, and feather in the touch-hole—and he was ready to shoot— to kill for the home skillet.

Having loaded his rifle just that way several thousand times in his life, he could do it in the dark or with his eyes shut. Once Abe took the gun as a flock of wild turkeys came toward the new log cabin, and, standing inside, shot through a crack and killed one of the big birds; and after that, somehow, he never felt like pulling the trigger on game-birds. A mile from the cabin was a salt lick where deer came; there the boy could have easily shot the animals, as they stood rubbing their tongues along the salty slabs or tasting of a saltish ooze. His father did the shooting; the deer killed gave them meat for Nancy's skillet; and the skins were tanned, cut, and stitched into shirts, trousers, mitts, moccasins. They wore buckskin; their valley was called the Buckhorn Valley.

After months the cabin stood up, four walls fitted together with a roof, a one-room house eighteen feet square, for a family to live in. A stick chimney plastered with clay ran up outside. The floor was packed and smoothed dirt. A log-fire lighted the inside; no windows were cut in the walls. For a door there was a hole cut to stoop through. Bedsteads were cleated to the corners of the cabin; pegs stuck in the side of a wall made a ladder for young Abe to climb up in a loft to sleep on a hump of dry leaves; rain and snow came through chinks of the roof onto his bearskin cover. A table and three-legged stools had the top sides smoothed with an ax, and the bark-side under, in the style called "puncheon."

A few days of this year in which the cabin was building, Nancy told Abe to wash his face and hands extra clean;

she combed his hair, held his face between her two hands, smacked him a kiss on the mouth, and sent him to school— nine miles and back—Abe and Sally hand in hand hiking eighteen miles a day. Tom Lincoln used to say Abe was going to have "a real eddication," explaining, "You air a-goin' to larn readin', writin', and cipherin'."

[84]

He learned to spell words he didn't know the meaning of, spelling the words before he used them in sentences. In a list of "words of eight syllables accented upon the sixth," was the word "incomprehensibility." He learned that first, and then such sentences as "Is he to go in?" and "Ann can spin flax."

Some neighbors said, "It's a pore make-out of a school," and Tom complained it was a waste of time to send the children nine miles just to sit with a lot of other children and read out loud all day in a "blab" school. But Nancy, as she cleaned Abe's ears in corners where he forgot to clean them, and as she combed out the tangles in his coarse, sandy black hair, used to say, "Abe, you go to school now, and larn all you kin." And he kissed her and said, "Yes, Mammy," and started with his sister on the nine-mile walk through timberland where bear, deer, coon, and wildcats ran wild.

Fall time came with its early frost and they were moved into the new cabin, when horses and a wagon came breaking into the clearing one day. It was Tom and Betsy Sparrow and their seventeen-year-old boy, Dennis Hanks, who had come from Hodgenville, Kentucky, to cook and sleep in the pole-shed of the Lincoln family till they could locate land and settle. Hardly a year had passed, however, when both Tom and Betsy Sparrow were taken down with the "milk sick," beginning with a whitish coat on the tongue. Both died and were buried in October on a little hill in a clearing in the timbers near by.

Soon after, there came to Nancy Hanks Lincoln that white coating of the tongue; her vitals burned; the tongue turned brownish; her feet and hands grew cold and colder, her pulse slow and slower. She knew she was dying, called for her children, and spoke to them her last choking words. Sarah and Abe leaned over the bed. A bony hand of the struggling mother went out, putting its fingers into the boy's sandy black hair; her fluttering guttural words seemed to say he must grow up and be good to his sister and father.

So, on a bed of poles cleated to the corner of the cabin, the body of Nancy Hanks Lincoln lay, looking tired . . . tired . . . with a peace settling in the pinched corners of the sweet, weary mouth, silence slowly etching away the lines of pain and hunger drawn around the gray eyes where now the eyelids closed down in the fine pathos of unbroken rest, a sleep without interruption settling about the form of the stooped and wasted shoulder-bones, looking to the children who tiptoed in, stood still, cried their tears of want and longing, whispered "Mammy, Mammy," and heard only their own whispers answering, looking to these little ones of her brood as though new secrets had come to her in place of the old secrets given up with the breath of life.

And Tom Lincoln took a log left over from the building of the cabin, and he and Dennis Hanks whipsawed the log into planks, planed the planks smooth, and made them of a measure for a box to bury the dead wife and mother in. Little Abe, with a jackknife, whittled pine-wood pegs. And then, while Dennis and Abe held the planks, Tom bored holes and stuck the whittled pegs through the bored holes. This was the coffin, and they carried it the next day to the same little timber clearing near by, where a few weeks before they had buried Tom and Betsy Sparrow. It was in the way of the deer-run leading to the saltish water; light feet and shy hoofs ran over those early winter graves.

So the woman, Nancy Hanks, died, thirty-six years old, a pioneer sacrifice, with memories of monotonous, endless everyday chores, of mystic Bible verses read over and over for their promises, and with memories of blue wistful hills and a summer when the crab-apple blossoms flamed white and she carried a boy-child into the world.

She had looked out on fields of blue-blossoming flax and hummed "Hey, Betty Martin, tiptoe, tiptoe"; she had sung of bright kingdoms by and by and seen the early frost

leaf its crystals on the stalks of buttonweed and redbud;
she had sung:

> You may bury me in the east,
> You may bury me in the west,
> And we'll all rise together in that morning.

CHAPTER XII

SOME weeks later, when David Elkin, elder of the Methodist church, was in that neighborhood, he was called on
to speak over the grave of Nancy Hanks. He had been acquainted with her in Kentucky, and to the Lincoln family
and a few neighbors he spoke of good things she had done,
sweet ways she had of living her life in this Vale of Tears,
and her faith in another life yonder past the River Jordan.

The "milk sick" took more people in that neighborhood
the same year, and Tom Lincoln whipsawed planks for
more coffins. One settler lost four milch cows and eleven

calves. The nearest doctor for people or cattle was thirty-five miles away. The wilderness is careless.

Lonesome and dark months came for Abe and Sarah. Worst of all were the weeks after their father went away, promising to come back.

Elizabethtown, Kentucky, was the place Tom Lincoln headed for. As he footed it through the woods and across the Ohio River, he was saying over to himself a speech— the words he would say to Sarah Bush Johnston, down in Elizabethtown. Her husband had died a few years before, and she was now in Tom's thoughts.

He went straight to the house where she was living in Elizabethtown, and, speaking to her as "Miss Johnston," he argued: "I have no wife and you no husband. I came a-purpose to marry you. I knowed you from a gal and you knowed me from a boy. I've no time to lose; and if you're willin' let it be done straight off."

Her answer was, "I got debts." She gave him a list of the debts; he paid them; a license was issued; and they were married on December 2, 1819.

He could write his name; she couldn't write hers. Trying to explain why the two of them took up with each other so quickly, Dennis Hanks at a later time said, "Tom had a kind o' way with women, an' maybe it was somethin' she took comfort in to have a man that didn't drink an' cuss none."

Little Abe and Sarah, living in the lonesome cabin on Little Pigeon Creek, Indiana, got a nice surprise one morning when four horses and a wagon came into their clearing, and their father jumped off, then Sarah Bush Lincoln, the new wife and mother, then John, Sarah, and Matilda Johnston, Sarah Bush's three children by her first husband. Next off the wagon came a feather mattress, feather pillows, a black walnut bureau, a large clothes-chest, a table, chairs, pots and skillets, knives, forks, spoons.

Abe ran his fingers over the slick wood of the bureau, pushed his fist into the feather pillows, sat in the new chairs, and wondered to himself, because this was the first time he had touched such fine things, such soft slick things.

"Here's your new mammy," his father told Abe as the boy looked up at a strong, large-boned, rosy woman, with a kindly face and eyes, with a steady voice, steady ways. The cheek-bones of her face stood out and she had a strong jaw-bone; she was warm and friendly for Abe's little hands to touch, right from the beginning. As one of her big hands held his head against her skirt he felt like a cold chick warming under the soft feathers of a big wing. She took the corn-husks Abe had been sleeping on, piled them in the yard and said they would be good for a pig-pen later on; and Abe sunk his head and bones that night in a feather pillow and a feather mattress.

Ten years pass with that cabin on Little Pigeon Creek for a home, and that farm and neighborhood the soil for growth. There the boy Abe grows to be the young man, Abraham Lincoln.

Ten years pass and the roots of a tree spread out finding water to carry up to branches and leaves that are in the sun; the trunk thickens, the forked limbs shine wider in the sun, they pray with their leaves in the rain and the whining wind; the tree arrives, the mystery of its coming, spreading, growing, a secret not even known to the tree itself; it stands with its arms stretched to the corners the four winds come from, with its murmured testimony, "We are here, we arrived, our roots are in the earth of these years," and beyond that short declaration, it speaks nothing of the decrees, fates, accidents, destinies, that made it an apparition of its particular moment.

Abe Lincoln grows up. His father talks about the waste of time in "eddication"; it is enough "to larn readin', writin', cipherin' "; but the stanch, yearning stepmother, Sarah Bush Lincoln, comes between the boy and the father. And the father listens to the stepmother and lets her have her way.

CHAPTER XIII

WHEN he was eleven years old, Abe Lincoln's young body began to change. The juices and glands began to make a long, tall boy out of him. As the months and years went by, he noticed his lean wrists getting longer, his legs too, and he was now looking over the heads of other boys. Men said, "Land o' Goshen, that boy air a-growin'!"

As he took on more length, they said he was shooting up into the air like green corn in the summer of a good corn-year. So he grew. When he reached seventeen years of age, and they measured him, he was six feet, nearly four inches, high, from the bottoms of his moccasins to the top of his skull.

These were years he was handling the ax. Except in spring plowing-time and the fall fodder-pulling, he was handling the ax nearly all the time. The insides of his hands took on callus thick as leather. He cleared openings in the timber, cut logs and puncheons, split fire-wood, built pig-pens.

He learned how to measure with his eye the half-circle swing of the ax so as to nick out the deepest possible chip from off a tree-trunk. The trick of swaying his body easily on the hips so as to throw the heaviest possible weight into the blow of the ax—he learned that.

On winter mornings he wiped the frost from the ax-handle, sniffed sparkles of air into his lungs, and beat a steady cleaving of blows into a big tree—till it fell—and he sat on the main log and ate his noon dinner of corn bread and fried salt pork—and joked with the gray squirrels that frisked and peeped at him from high forks of near-by walnut trees.

He learned how to make his ax flash and bite into a sugar-maple or a sycamore. The outside and the inside look of black walnut and black oak, hickory and jack oak, elm and white oak, sassafras, dogwood, grapevines, sumac—he came on their secrets. He could guess close to the time of

[94]

the year, to the week of the month, by the way the leaves and branches of trees looked. He sniffed the seasons.

Often he worked alone in the timbers, all day long with only the sound of his own ax, or his own voice speaking to himself, or the crackling and swaying of branches in the wind, and the cries and whirs of animals, of brown and silver-gray squirrels, of partridges, hawks, crows, turkeys, sparrows, and the occasional wildcats.

The tricks and whimsies of the sky, how to read clear skies and cloudy weather, the creeping vines of ivy and wild grape, the recurrence of dogwood blossoms in spring, the ways of snow, rain, drizzle, sleet, the visitors of sky and weather coming and going hour by hour—he tried to read their secrets, he tried to be friendly with their mystery.

So he grew, to become hard, tough, wiry. The muscle on his bones and the cords, tendons, cross-weaves of fiber, and nerve centers, these became instruments to obey his wishes. He found with other men he could lift his own end of a log—and more too. One of the neighbors said he was strong as three men. Another said, "He can sink an ax deeper into wood than any man I ever saw." And another, "If you heard him fellin' trees in a clearin', you would say there was three men at work by the way the trees fell."

He was more than a tough, long, rawboned boy. He

[95]

amazed men with his man's lifting power. He put his shoulders under a new-built corncrib one day and walked away with it to where the farmer wanted it. Four men, ready with poles to put under it and carry it, didn't need their poles. He played the same trick with a chicken house; at the new, growing town of Gentryville near by, they said the chicken house weighed six hundred pounds, and only a big boy with a hard backbone could get under it and walk away with it.

A blacksmith shop, a grocery, and a store had started up on the crossroads of the Gentry farm. And one night after Abe had been helping thresh wheat on Dave Turnham's place, he went with Dennis Hanks, John Johnston, and some other boys to Gentryville where the farm-hands sat around with John Baldwin, the blacksmith, and Jones, the storekeeper, passed the whisky jug, told stories, and talked politics and religion and gossip. Going home late that night, they saw something in a mud puddle alongside the road. They stepped over to see whether it was a man or a hog. It was a man—drunk—snoring—sleeping off his drunk—on a frosty night outdoors in a cold wind.

They shook him by the shoulders, doubled his knees to his stomach, but he went on sleeping, snoring. The cold wind was getting colder. The other boys said they were going home, and they went away leaving Abe alone with

[96]

the snoring sleeper in the mud puddle. Abe stepped into the mud, reached arms around the man, slung him over his shoulders, carried him to Dennis Hanks's cabin, built a fire, rubbed him warm and left him sleeping off the whisky.

And the man afterward said Abe saved his life. He told John Hanks, "It was mighty clever of Abe to tote me to a warm fire that night."

So he grew, living in that Pigeon Creek cabin for a home, sleeping in the loft, climbing up at night to a bed just under the roof, where sometimes the snow and the rain drove through the cracks, eating sometimes at a table where the family had only one thing to eat—potatoes. Once at the table, when there were only potatoes, his father spoke a blessing to the Lord for potatoes; the boy murmured, "Those are mighty poor blessings." And Abe made jokes once when company came and Sally Bush Lincoln brought out raw potatoes, gave the visitors a knife apiece, and they all peeled raw potatoes, and talked about the crops, politics, religion, gossip.

Days when they had only potatoes to eat didn't come often. Other days in the year they had "yaller-legged chicken" with gravy, and corn dodgers with shortening, and berries and honey. They tasted of bear meat, deer, coon, quail, grouse, prairie turkey, catfish, bass, perch.

Abe knew the sleep that comes after long hours of work outdoors, the feeling of simple food changing into blood and muscle as he worked in those young years clearing timberland for pasture and corn crops, cutting loose the brush, piling it and burning it, splitting rails, pulling the crosscut saw and the whipsaw, driving the shovel-plow, harrowing, planting, hoeing, pulling fodder, milking cows, churning butter, helping neighbors at house-raisings, log-rollings, corn-huskings.

He found he was fast, strong, and keen when he went against other boys in sports. On farms where he worked, he held his own at scuffling, knocking off hats, wrestling. The time came when around Gentryville and Spencer County he was known as the best "rassler" of all, the champion. In jumping, foot-racing, throwing the maul, pitching the crowbar, he carried away the decisions against the lads of his own age always, and usually won against those older than himself.

He earned his board, clothes, and lodgings, sometimes working for a neighbor farmer. He watched his father, while helping make cabinets, coffins, cupboards, window frames, doors. Hammers, saws, pegs, cleats, he understood first-hand, also the scythe and the cradle for cutting hay and grain, the corn-cutter's knife, the leather piece to protect the hand while shucking corn, and the horse, the dog, the cow, the ox, the hog. He could skin and cure the hides of coon and deer. He lifted the slippery two-hundred-pound hog carcass, head down, holding the hind hocks up for others of the gang to hook, and swung the animal clear of the ground. He learned where to stick a hog in the under side of the neck so as to bleed it to death, how to split it in two, and carve out the chops, the parts for sausage grinding, for hams, for "cracklings."

Farmers called him to butcher for them at thirty-one cents a day, this when he was sixteen and seventeen years old. He could "knock a beef in the head," swing a maul and hit a cow between the eyes, skin the hide, halve and quarter it, carve out the tallow, the steaks, kidneys, liver.

And the hiding-places of fresh spring water under the earth crust had to be in his thoughts; he helped at well-digging; the wells Tom Lincoln dug went dry one year after another; neighbors said Tom was always digging a well and had his land "honeycombed"; and the boy, Abe, ran the errands and held the tools for the well-digging.

When he was eighteen years old, he could take an ax at the end of the handle and hold it out in a straight horizontal line, easy and steady—he had strong shoulder muscles and steady wrists early in life. He walked thirty-four miles in one day, just on an errand, to please himself, to hear a lawyer make a speech. He could tell his body to do almost impossible things, and the body obeyed.

Growing from boy to man, he was alone a good deal of the time. Days came often when he was by himself all the time except at breakfast and supper hours in the cabin home. In some years more of his time was spent in loneliness than in the company of other people. It happened, too, that this loneliness he knew was not like that of people in cities who can look from a window on streets where faces pass and repass. It was the wilderness loneliness he became acquainted with, solved, filtered through body, eye, and brain, held communion with in his ears, in the temples of his forehead, in the works of his beating heart.

He lived with trees, with the bush wet with shining raindrops, with the burning bush of autumn, with the lone wild duck riding a north wind and crying down on a line north to south, the faces of open sky and weather, the ax which is an individual one-man instrument, these he had for companions, books, friends, talkers, chums of his endless changing soliloquies.

His moccasin feet in the winter-time knew the white spaces of snowdrifts piled in whimsical shapes against timber slopes or blown in levels across the fields of last year's cut corn stalks; in the summer-time his bare feet toughened in the gravel of green streams while he laughed back to the chatter of bluejays in the red-haw trees or while he kept his eyes ready in the slough quack-grass for the cow-snake, the rattler, the copperhead.

He rested between spells of work in the springtime when the upward push of the coming out of the new grass can be heard, and in autumn weeks when the rustle of a single falling leaf lets go a whisper that a listening ear can catch.

He found his life thrown in ways where there was a certain chance for a certain growth. And so he grew. Silence found him; he met silence. In the making of him as he was, the element of silence was immense.

CHAPTER XIV

I⟨ᴛ⟩ was a little country of families living in one-room cabins. Dennis Hanks said at a later time, "We lived the same as the Indians, 'ceptin' we took an interest in politics and religion."

Cash was scarce; venison hams, bacon slabs, and barrels of whisky served as money; there were seasons when store-keepers asked customers, "What kind of money have you today?" because so many sorts of wildcat dollar bills were passing around. In sections of timberland, wild hogs were nosing out a fat living on hickory nuts, walnuts, acorns; it was said the country would be full of wild hogs if the wolves didn't find the litters of young pigs a few weeks old and kill them.

Farmers lost thirty and forty sheep in a single wolf raid. Toward the end of June came "fly time," when cows lost weight and gave less milk because they had to fight flies. For two or three months at the end of summer, horses weakened, unless covered with blankets, under the attacks of horse-flies; where one lighted on a horse, a drop of blood oozed; horses were hitched to branches of trees that gave loose rein to the animals, room to move and fight flies.

Men and women went barefoot except in the colder weather; women carried their shoes in their hands and put them on just before arrival at church meetings or at social parties.

Rains came, loosening the top soil of the land where it was not held by grass roots; it was a yellow clay that softened to slush; in this yellow slush many a time Abe Lincoln walked ankle-deep; his bare feet were intimate with the clay dust of the hot dog-days, with the clay mud of spring and fall rains; he was at home in clay. In the timbers with his ax, on the way to chop, his toes, heels, soles, the balls of his feet, climbed and slid in banks and sluices of clay. In the corn-fields, plowing, hoeing, cutting, and shucking, again his bare feet spoke with the clay of the earth; it was in his toenails and stuck on the skin of his toe-knuckles. The color of clay was one of his own colors.

In the short and simple annals of the poor, it seems there are people who breathe with the earth and take into their lungs and blood some of the hard and dark strength of its mystery. During six and seven months each year in the twelve fiercest formative years of his life, Abraham Lincoln had the pads of his foot-soles bare against clay of the earth. It may be the earth told him in her own tough gypsy slang one or two knacks of living worth keeping. To be organic with running wildfire and quiet rain, both of the same moment, is to be the carrier of wave-lines the earth gives up only on hard usage.

CHAPTER XV

HE took shape in a tall, long-armed cornhusker. When rain came in at the chinks of the cabin loft where he slept, soaking through the book Josiah Crawford loaned him, he pulled fodder two days to pay for the book, made a clean sweep, till there wasn't a blade left on a cornstalk in the field of Josiah Crawford.

His father was saying the big boy looked as if he had been roughhewn with an ax and needed smoothing with a jack-plane. "He was the ganglin'est, awkwardest feller that ever stepped over a ten-rail snake fence; he had t' duck to git through a door; he 'peared to be all j'ints."

His stepmother told him she didn't mind his bringing dirt into the house on his feet; she could scour the floor; but she asked him to keep his head washed or he'd be rubbing the dirt on her nice whitewashed rafters. He put barefoot boys to wading in a mud-puddle near the horse-trough, picked them up one by one, carried them to the house upside down, and walked their muddy feet across the ceiling. The mother came in, laughed an hour at the foot-tracks, told Abe he ought to be spanked—and he cleaned the ceiling so it looked new.

The mother said, "Abe never spoke a cross word to me in his life since we lived together." And she said Abe was truthful; when Tilda Johnston leaped onto Abe's back to give him a scare on a lonely timber path, she brought the big axman to the ground by pulling her hands against his shoulders and pressing her knee into his backbone. The ax-blade cut her ankle, and strips from Abe's shirt and Tilda's dress had to be used to stop the blood. By then she was sobbing over what to tell her mother. On Abe's advice she told her mother the whole truth.

As time went by, the stepmother of Abe became one of the rich, silent forces in his life. Besides keeping the floors, pots, pans, kettles, and milk-crocks spick and span, weaving, sewing, mending, and managing with sagacity and gumption, she had a massive, bony, human strength backed with an elemental faith that the foundations of the world were mortised by God with unspeakable goodness of heart toward the human family. Hard as life was, she was thankful to be alive.

Once she told Abe how her brother Isaac, back in Hardin County, had hot words with a cowardly young man who shot Isaac without warning. The doctors asked Isaac if they could tie him down while they cut his flesh and took out the bullet. He told them he didn't need to be tied down; he put two lead musket-balls in between his teeth and ground his teeth on them while the doctors cut a slash nine inches long and one inch deep till they found the bullet and brought it out. Isaac never let out a moan or a whimper; he set his teeth into the musket-balls, ground them into flat sheets, and spat them from his mouth when he thanked the doctors.

Sally Bush, the stepmother, was all of a good mother to Abe. If he broke out laughing when others saw nothing to laugh at, she let it pass as a sign of his thoughts working their own way. So far as she was concerned he had a right to do unaccountable things; since he never lied to her, why not? So she justified him. When Abe's sister, Sarah, mar-

ried Aaron Grigsby and a year after died with her newborn child, it was Sally Bush who spoke comfort to the
eighteen-year-old boy of Nancy Hanks burying his sister
and the wraith of a child.

A neighbor woman sized him up by saying, "He could
work when he wanted to, but he was no hand to pitch in
like killing snakes." John Romine made the remarks:
"Abe Lincoln worked for me, but was always reading and
thinking. I used to get mad at him for it. I say he was
awful lazy. He would laugh and talk—crack his jokes and
tell stories all the time; didn't love work half as much as
his pay. He said to me one day that his father taught him to
work, but he never taught him to love it."

A misunderstanding came up one time between Abe Lincoln and William Grigsby. It ended with Grigsby so mad
he challenged Abe to a fight. Abe looked down at Grigsby,
smiled, and said the fight ought to be with John Johnston,
Abe's stepbrother. The day was set for the fight; each man
was there with his seconds; the mauling began, with the
two fighters stripped to the waist, beating and bruising
each other with bare knuckles.

A crowd stood around, forming a ring, cheering, yell-
ing, hissing, till after a while they saw Johnston getting the
worst of it. Then the ring of people forming the crowd

PIONEER PLAY

was broken as Abe Lincoln shouldered his way through, stepped out, took hold of Grigsby and threw that fighter out of the center of the fight-ring.

Then Abe Lincoln called out, "I'm the big buck of this lick." And looking around so his eyes swept the circle of the crowd he let loose the challenge, "If any of you want to try it, come on and whet your horns." A riot of wild fist-fighting came then between the two gangs and for months around the Jones grocery store there was talk about which gang whipped the other.

After a fox-chase with horses, Uncle Jimmy Larkin was telling how his horse won the race, was the best horse in the world, and never drew a long breath; Abe didn't listen; Uncle Jimmy told it again, and Abe said, "Why don't you tell us how many short breaths he drew?" It raised a laugh on Jimmy, who jumped around threatening to fight, till Abe said quietly, "Now, Larkin, if you don't shut up I'll throw you in that water."

Asked by Farmer James Taylor if he could kill a hog, he answered, "If you will risk the hog I'll risk myself."

He had the pride of youth that resents the slur, the snub, besides the riotous blood that has always led youth in reck-less exploits. When he was cutting up didos one day at the Crawford farm-house, Mrs. Crawford asked, "What's going to become of you, Abe?" And with mockery of swagger, he answered, "Me? I'm going to be president of the United States."

Driving a horse at the mill, he was sending the whip-lash over the nag and calling, "Git up, you old hussy; git up, you old hussy." The horse let fly a hind foot that knocked down the big boy just as he yelled, "Git up." He lay bleeding, was taken home, washed, put to bed, and lay all night unconscious. As his eye winkers opened the next day and he came to, his tongue struggled and blurted, "You old hussy," thus finishing what he started to say before the knockdown.

CHAPTER XVI

A MILE across the fields from the Lincoln home was the
Pigeon church, a log-built meeting-house put up in 1822
after many discussions among members about where to
locate. On June 7, 1823, William Barker, who kept the
minutes and records, wrote that the church "received
Brother Thomas Lincoln by letter." He was elected the
next year with two neighbors to serve as a committee of
visitors to the Gilead church, and served three years as
church trustee. Strict watch was kept on the conduct of
members and Tom served on committees to look into re-
ported misconduct between husbands and wives, brothers
and sisters, of neighbor against neighbor.

William Barker once entered the subscriptions for the
support of the church as follows: "We the undersined do
asign our names to pay the sevrial somes annexed to our
names in produce this fall to be delivered betwixt the first
and 20th of December the produce is as follows corn wheat

whiskey pork Linnen wool or any other article or material to do the work with. the produce will be Dilevered at the meting hoas in good marchanable produce." Among the subscribers was recorded, "undersined"—"Thomas Lincoln in corn manufactured pounds 24."

Along with the earliest settlers in Indiana had come Catholic priests, and Baptist and Presbyterian preachers, and Methodist circuit riders. Churches had been organized, and the members, with prayer and songs, hewed the logs and raised the frames of their meeting-houses for worship. Time had been when the circuit-rider traveled with Bible in one hand and rifle in the other, preaching to members, sinners, and "scorners" in settlers' cabins or in timber groves. To the members, the Bible, and the lands, names, stories, texts, and teachings of the Bible, were overshadowing realities, to be read, thought over, interpreted, and used in daily life. To "grow in grace" and to arrive at "grace abounding," to be "strong in sperrit," to "cast out delusion," were matters connected definitely with the daily life of arising, building a fire, breaking the ice sheets on water, and starting a kettle to boil, and then going forth to the chores of the barn and the horse-trough, the corncrib, the pigpen. Such biblical words as "malice," "mercy," and "charity" were topics of long explanations.

Most of the church people could read only the shortest

words in the Bible, or none at all. They sat in the log meeting-house on the split-log benches their own axes had
shaped, listening to the preacher reading from the Bible
by the light of fire-logs. The pronunciation of the words
Egypt, Mesopotamia, Babylon, Damascus, set minds to
work imagining places less real to them than Rockport,
Boonville, Vincennes, Cincinnati. Epithets and texts enun-
ciated often by preachers became tissues of their spiritual
lives; the words meant something beyond the actual words
in "weeping and wailing and gnashing of teeth," "an eye
for an eye, and a tooth for a tooth," "by the waters of
Babylon." They could see the direct inference to be drawn
from, "The fathers have eaten sour grapes and the children's teeth are set on edge," or the suggestions in "Let not
your heart be troubled," or "Let him who is without sin
cast the first stone," or "As ye would that others should do
unto you, do ye even so unto them."

Their own morning-glories, honeysuckle, and blooming
perennials came to leafage out of the rhythmic text, "Con-
sider the lilies of the field, how they grow; they toil not,
neither do they spin; and yet I say unto you, that even
Solomon in all his glory was not arrayed like one of these."
They felt enough portents in the two words, "Jesus wept,"
for the arrangement of that as a verse by itself.

At the Pigeon church one of the favorite hymns was

"How Tedious and Tasteless the Hours," and another, "Oh, to Grace How Great a Debtor!" and another began with the lines:

> When I can read my title clear
> To mansions in the skies.

To confess, to work hard, to be saving, to be decent, were the actions most praised and pleaded for in the sermons of the preachers. Next to denying Christ, the worst sins were drinking, gambling, fighting, loafing, among the men, and gossiping, back-biting, sloth, and slack habits, among the women. A place named Hell where men, women, and children burned everlastingly in fires was the place where sinners would go.

In a timber grove one summer Sunday afternoon, a preacher yelled, shrieked, wrung his hands in sobs of hysterics, until a row of women were laid out to rest and recover in the shade of an oak-tree, after they had moaned, shaken, danced up and down, worn themselves out with "the jerks" and fainted. And young Abe Lincoln, looking on, with sober face and quiet heart, was thoughtful about what he saw before his eyes.

The Sabbath was not only a day for religious meetings. After the sermon, the members, who rode horses many miles to the meeting-house, talked about crops, weather, births and deaths, the growing settlements, letters just come, politics, Indians, and land-titles.

Families had prayers in the morning on arising, grace at breakfast, noon prayers and grace at dinner, grace at supper, and evening prayers at bedtime. In those households, the manger at Bethlehem was a white miracle, the Black Friday at Golgotha and the rocks rolled away for the Resurrection were near-by realities of terror and comfort, dark power and sustenance. The Sabbath day, Christmas, Easter, were days for sober thoughts and sober faces, resignation, contemplation, rest, silence. Verses in the Gospel of St. John had rhythm and portent. "I am the way, the truth, and the life. . . . He that believeth in me shall not perish but shall have everlasting life."

Besides a wisdom of short syllables covering all the wants of life in the Lord's Prayer, they found a melodious movement of musical intention in the arrangement of its simple words. It was like a walk from a green valley to a great mountain to pronounce with thoughtful cadence: "Give us this day our daily bread. And forgive us our trespasses as we forgive those who trespass against us. And lead us not into temptation but deliver us from evil."

The glisten of dewdrops on wheat straws, in the gray chill of daybreak on harvest fields, shone in the solemn assurance of, "Yea, though I walk through the valley of the shadow of death, I will fear no evil: . . . thy rod and thy staff they comfort me."

There was occupation of the imaginative gift, a challenge even to the sleeping or crying senses of color and form, hidden in the picture of Jacob's ladder stretching from the man in earth-slumber up beyond the limits of sky; in the drama of Jonah entering the belly of the whale and later issuing forth from that darkness; in the swift stride of the four horsemen of the apocalypse; in the coat of many colors worn by Joseph and the dream of seven years of famine to come upon Egypt; in the flawless and clear-eyed sheep-boy David, walking with sling and stone to win battle against the stiff-necked giant Goliath by reason of one fierce stone pounded home to the forehead of the swaggerer; in the massive prefigurements of preparation for calamity or destruction of mortal pride to be found in the episodes of Noah's ark and the upthrust and comedown of the Tower of Babel.

After a day of plowing corn, watching crop pests, whittling bean-poles, capturing strayed cattle and fixing up a hole in a snake-rail fence, while the housewife made a kettle of soap, hoed the radishes and cabbages, milked the cows, and washed the baby, there was a consolation leading to easy slumber in the beatitudes: "Blessed are the meek: for they shall inherit the earth. . . . Blessed are the pure in heart, for they shall see God. Blessed are the peace-makers: for they shall be called the children of God." It was not their business to be sure of the arguments and the invincible logic that might underlie the Bible promises of heaven and threats of hell; it was for this the preacher was hired and paid by the corn, wheat, whisky, pork, linen, wool, and other produce brought by the members of the church.

The exquisite foretokening, "In my Father's house are many mansions: if it were not so I would have told you," was but a carrying farther of the implications of that cry from the ramparts of the unconquerable, "O death, where is thy sting? O grave, where is thy victory?"

Beyond Indiana was something else; beyond the timber and underbrush, the malaria, milk-sick, blood, sweat, tears, hands hard and crooked as the roots of walnut trees, there must be something else.

Young Abraham Lincoln saw certain of these Christians with a clean burning fire, with inner reckonings that prompted them to silence or action or speech, and they could justify themselves with a simple and final explanation that all things should be done decently and in order. Their door-strings were out to sinners deep in mire, to scorners seemingly past all redemption; the Jesus who lived with lawbreakers, thieves, lepers crying "Unclean!"

was an instrument and a light vivifying into everyday use the abstractions behind the words "malice," "mercy," "charity."

They met understanding from the solemn young Lincoln who had refused to join his schoolmates in torturing a live mud-turtle, and had written a paper arguing against cruelty to animals; who when eleven years old took his father's rifle and shot a prairie turkey and had never since shot any game at all; who could butcher a beef or hog for food but didn't like to see rabbit blood; who wanted to be a river steamboat pilot but gave up in simple obedience when his father told him he was needed at home; who as a nine-year-old boy helped get a traveling preacher to speak some sort of final ceremonial words over the winter grave of Nancy Hanks Lincoln; who would bother to lug on his shoulders and save from freezing the body of a man overloaded with whisky; who had seen one of his companions go insane and who used to get up before daylight and cross the fields to listen to the crooning, falsetto cackling, and disconnected babbling of one whose brain had suddenly lost control of things done decently and in order.

The footsteps of death, silent as the moving sundial of a tall sycamore, were a presence. Time and death, the partners who operate leaving no more track than mist, had to be reckoned in the scheme of life. A day is a shooting-star. The young Lincoln tried to rhyme this sentiment:

> Time! what an empty vapor 'tis!
> And days how swift they are:
> Swift as an Indian arrow—
> Fly on like a shooting star,
> The present moment just is here,
> Then slides away in haste,
> That we can never say they're ours,
> But only say they're past.

His mother Nancy Hanks and her baby that didn't live, his sister Sarah and her baby that didn't live—time and the empty vapor had taken them; the rain and the snow beat on their graves. The young man who was in his right mind and then began babbling week in and week out the droolings of a disordered brain—time had done it without warning. On both man and the animals, time and death had their way. In a single week, the milk-sick had taken four milch-cows and eleven calves of Dennis Hanks, while Dennis too had nearly gone under with a hard week of it.

At the Pigeon Creek settlement, while the structure of his bones, the build and hang of his torso and limbs, took shape, other elements, invisible, yet permanent, traced their lines in the tissues of his head and heart.

CHAPTER XVII

PIONEERS are half gypsy. The lookout is on horizons from which at any time another and stranger wandersong may come calling and take the heart, to love or to kill, with gold or with ashes, with bluebirds burbling in ripe cornfields or with rheumatism or hog cholera or mortgages, rust and bugs eating crops and farms into ruin.

They are luck-hunters. And luck—is it *yonder?* Over the horizon, over yonder—is there a calling and a calling? The pioneers, so often, are believers in luck . . . out yonder.

And always the worker on land, who puts in crops and bets on the weather and gambles in seed corn and hazards his toil against so many whimsical, fateful conditions, has a pull on his heart to believe he can read luck signs, and tell good luck or bad luck to come, in dreams of his sleep at night, in changes of the moon, in the manners of chickens and dogs, in little seeming accidents that reveal the intentions and operations of forces beyond sight and smell.

They have noticed certain coincidences operating to produce certain results in the past. And when again those coincidences arise they say frankly, "I'm superstitious— what happened before is liable to happen again." The simple saying among simple people, "If a bird lights in a window there will be a death in that house," goes back to the fact that there have been deaths, and many of them, in houses to which a bird came and sat on a window-sill and picked his wings and put on dark assumptions.

Down in Indiana, as Abe Lincoln grew up, he cherished his sweet dreams, and let the bitter ones haunt him, and tried to search out from the muddled hugger-mugger of still other dreams whether the meaning was to be sweet or bitter. His father had had portentous dreams; his father told how in a night's sleep once he saw a wayside path to a strange house; he saw the inside walls, the chairs, the table, the fireplace in that house; at the fireside a woman was sitting, and her face, eyes, and lips came clear; she was paring an apple; she was the woman to be his wife. This was the dream, and in his night's sleep it came again and again; he could not shake it off. It haunted him till he went to the path, followed the path to the house, went inside and there saw the woman, sitting at the fireside paring an apple; her face, eyes, and lips were those he had seen so often in his night sleep; and the rest of his dream came to pass. Tom Lincoln had told this to his son, Abe, and the boy searched his dreams for meanings. He learned to say of certain coincidences, "I'm superstitious," feeling that what had happened before under certain combinations of events would probably happen again.

Even the water underground, the streams and springs, were whimsical, unreliable, ran by luck, it seemed, in southern Indiana. Not far from the Lincolns was a region where rivers dipped down into limestone and faded out of sight. "Lost rivers," they were called. In Wyandotte Cave a walker could go fifteen miles around the inside. In some counties there was no telling when a good well would give out and say, "No more water here."

Abe's father hired a man to come with a witch-hazel and tell by the way the magic stick pointed where to dig a well that wouldn't go dry. The well was dug where the witch-hazel said it should be dug. And that well went dry just as others before had on the Lincoln farm.

Besides superstitions there were sayings, to be spoken and guessed about, old pieces of whim and wisdom out of bygone generations of Kentuckians, of English, Scotch, and Irish souls. Potatoes, growing underground, must be planted in the dark of the moon, while beans, growing above-ground, must be planted in the light of the moon. The posts of a rail fence would sink in the ground if not set in the dark of the moon. Trees for rails must be cut in the early part of the day and in the light of the moon. If in planting corn you skipped a row there would be a death in the family. If you killed the first snake you saw in the spring, you would win against all your enemies that year. If rheumatism came, skunk-grease or red worm-oil rubbed where the ache was would cure it.

Steal a dishrag, people said, and hide it in a tree-stump and your wart will go away. If you have many warts, tie as many knots in a string as there are warts, and bury the string under a stone. A dog crossing a hunter's path means bad luck unless he hooks his two little fingers together and pulls till the dog is out of sight. Feed gunpowder to dogs and it will make them fierce. To start on a journey and see a white mule is bad luck. If a horse breathes on a child, the child will have the whooping-cough. Buckeyes carried in the pocket keep off the rheumatism.

When a man is putting up a crop of hay or shucking a field of corn or driving a load of wood, the weather has a particular interest for him. Out of the lives of farmers, timber-workers, ox-drivers, in Kentucky and Indiana, have come sayings:

If the sun shines while it is raining, it will rain again the next day; birds and hens singing during the rain indicate fair weather; if roosters crow when they go to roost it is a sign of rain; the first thunder in the spring wakes up the snakes from their winter sleep; when chickens get on a fence during a rain and pick themselves, it is a sign of clear weather; when the rain gets thick and heavy, almost like mist, it will turn cold; if a bobwhite says bob only once there will be rain; rain from the east rains three days at least; if it rains before seven it will clear before eleven; if there is lightning in the north it will rain in twenty-four hours; lightning in the south means dry weather.

"If a man can't skin he must hold a leg while some one else does," was a saying among the butcher gangs Abe Lincoln worked with. Men in those gangs would indicate a short distance by saying it was "far as you can throw a bull by the tail." A strong whisky "would make a rabbit spit in a dog's face." There were admonitions: "Spit against the wind and you spit in your own face," or "Don't see all you see, and don't hear all you hear."

Then, too, there were sayings spoken among the men only, out of barn-life and handling cattle and hogs; the daily chores required understanding of the necessary habits of men and animals.

And naturally in field and kitchen, among young and old, there were the phrases and epithets, "as plain as the nose on your face; as easy as licking a dish; as welcome as the flowers in May; as bare as the back of my hand; before the cat can lick her ear; as red as a spanked baby."

And there were eloquent Irish with blessings, maledictions, and proverbs. "Better be red-headed than be without a head." "No man can live longer at peace than his neighbors like." "I think his face is made of a fiddle; every one that looks on him loves him." "She's as dirty as a slut that's too lazy to lick herself." "A liar must have a good memory." "It's an ill fight where he that wins has the worst of it." "Hills look green that are far away." "It will be all the same after you're dead a hundred years."

Among the young people were whimsies often spoken and seldom believed. Fancy was on a loose leash in some of these. "If you can make your first and little finger meet over the back of your hand, you will marry." "If you spit on a chunk of firewood and speak your sweetheart's name, he will come before it burns out." "The new moon must never be seen through the trees when making a wish." "If a butterfly comes into the house a lady will call wearing a dress the color of the butterfly." "If you sing before breakfast you will cry before night." "If the fire roars there will be a quarrel in the family."

"If two hens fight in the barnyard there will be two ladies calling." "If your ears burn somebody is gossiping about you." "If your hand itches you will get a present or shake hands with a stranger; if your right foot itches you are going on a journey; if the left foot itches you are going where you are not wanted; if your nose itches away from home you are wanted at home, but if your nose itches at home some one is coming to see you; if your right eye itches you will cry and if it is the left eye you will laugh." "If you break a looking-glass you will have seven years of bad luck." "If you let a baby under a year old look in the mirror it will die." "It is bad luck to step over a broom."

Among the games played at parties by the young people in Indiana was the farm classic "Skip to My Lou" which tells of a little red wagon painted blue, a mule in the cellar kicking up through, chickens in the haystack shoo shoo shoo, flies in the cream jar shoo shoo shoo, rabbits in the bean patch two by two.

> Hurry up slow poke, do oh do,
> Hurry up slow poke, do oh do,
> Hurry up slow poke, do oh do,
> Skip to my Lou, my darling.
>
> I'll get her back in spite of you,
> I'll get her back in spite of you,
> I'll get her back in spite of you,
> Skip to my Lou, my darling.

SKIP TO MY LOU

Gone again, what shall I do?
Gone again, what shall I do?
Gone again, what shall I do?
Skip to my Lou, my darling.

I'll get another one sweeter than you,
I'll get another one sweeter than you,
I'll get another one sweeter than you,
Skip to my Lou, my darling.

And there were other classics such as "Way Down in the Pawpaw Patch," "All Chaw Hay on the Corner," "Pig in the Parlor," "Old Bald Eagle, Sail Around," and "Pop Goes the Weasel." The game of "Old Sister Phoebe," with a quaint British strain, had song couplets:

Old Sister Phoebe, how merry were we,
The night we sat under the juniper tree,
The juniper tree, high-o, high-o,
The juniper tree, high-o.

Take this hat on your head, keep your head warm,
And take a sweet kiss, it will do you no harm.

It will do you no harm, but a great deal of good,
And so take another while kissing goes good.

In "Thus the Farmer Sows His Seed," an ancient human dialogue is rehearsed:

Come, my love, and go with me,
And I will take good care of thee.

I am too young, I am not fit.
I cannot leave my mamma yet.

You're old enough, you are just right,
I asked your mamma last Saturday night.

Among a people who spun their own wool and wove
their own cloth, as their forefathers had done, there was
the inheritance of the game of "Weevily Wheat," danced
somewhat like the Virginia Reel, with singing passages:

O Charley, he's a fine young man,
O Charley, he's a dandy,
He loves to hug and kiss the girls,
And feed 'em on good candy.

The higher up the cherry tree,
The riper grow the cherries,
The more you hug and kiss the girls,
The sooner they will marry.

My pretty little pink, I suppose you think
I care but little about you.
But I'll let you know before you go,
I cannot do without you.

It's left hand round your weevily wheat.
It's both hands round your weevily wheat.
Come down this way with your weevily wheat.
It's swing, oh, swing, your weevily wheat.

NEIGHBORHOOD FAVORITES

Among the best-remembered favorites in the neighborhood around the Lincoln farm in Indiana were "Skip to My Lou," "Old Sister Phoebe," "Thus the Farmer Sows His Seed," and "Weevily Wheat."

They had patriotic songs for the Fourth of July, chief of which was "Hail Columbia," printed as follows:

Hail! Columbia, happy land!
Hail! ye heroes, heav'n-born band,
Who faught and bled in freedom's cause,
Who faught, &c.

And when the storm of war is gone,
Enjoy the peace your valor won;
Let independence be your boast,
Ever mindful what it cost,
Ever grateful for the prize,
May its altar reach the skies.

CHAPTER XVIII

THE farm boys in their evenings at Jones's store in Gentryville talked about how Abe Lincoln was always reading,
digging into books, stretching out flat on his stomach in
front of the fireplace, studying till midnight and past midnight, picking a piece of charcoal to write on the fire
shovel, shaving off what he wrote, and then writing more
—till midnight and past midnight. The next thing Abe
would be reading books between the plow handles, it
seemed to them. And once trying to speak a last word,

Dennis Hanks said, "There's suthin' peculiarsome about Abe."

He wanted to learn, to know, to live, to reach out; he wanted to satisfy hungers and thirsts he couldn't tell about, this big boy of the backwoods. And some of what he wanted so much, so deep down, seemed to be in the books. Maybe in books he would find the answers to dark questions pushing around in the pools of his thoughts and the drifts of his mind. He told Dennis and other people, "The things I want to know are in books; my best friend is the man who'll git me a book I ain't read." And sometimes friends answered, "Well, books ain't as plenty as wildcats in these parts o' Indianny."

This was one thing meant by Dennis when he said there was "suthin' peculiarsome" about Abe. It seemed that Abe made the books tell him more than they told other people. All the other farm boys had gone to school and read "The Kentucky Preceptor," but Abe picked out questions from it, such as "Who has the most right to complain, the Indian or the negro?" and Abe would talk about it, up one way and down the other, while they were in the cornfield pulling fodder for the winter. When Abe got hold of a storybook and read about a boat that came near a magnetic rock, and how the magnets in the rock pulled all the nails out of the boat so it went to pieces and the people in the boat found themselves floundering in water, Abe thought it was funny and told it to other people. After Abe read poetry, especially Bobby Burns's poems, Abe began writing rhymes himself. When Abe sat with a girl, with their bare feet in the creek water, and she spoke of the moon rising, he explained to her it was the earth moving and not the moon—the moon only seemed to rise.

John Hanks, who worked in the fields barefooted with Abe, grubbing stumps, plowing, mowing, said: "When Abe and I came back to the house from work, he used to go to the cupboard, snatch a piece of corn bread, sit down, take a book, cock his legs up high as his head, and read. Whenever Abe had a chance in the field while at work, or at the house, he would stop and read." He liked to explain to other people what he was getting from books; explaining an idea to some one else made it clearer to him. The habit was growing on him of reading out loud; words came more real if picked from the silent page of the book and pronounced on the tongue; new balances and values of words stood out if spoken aloud. When writing letters for his father or the neighbors, he read the words out loud as they got written. Before writing a letter he asked questions such as: "What do you want to say in the letter? How do you want to say it? Are you sure that's the best way to say it? Or do you think we can fix up a better way to say it?"

As he studied his books his lower lip stuck out; Josiah Crawford noticed it was a habit and joked Abe about the "stuck-out lip." This habit too stayed with him.

He wrote in his Sum Book or arithmetic that Compound Division was "When several numbers of Divers Denominations are given to be divided by 1 common divisor," and worked on the exercise in multiplication; "If 1 foot contain 12 inches I demand how many there are in 126 feet." Thus the schoolboy.

What he got in the schools didn't satisfy him. He went to three different schools in Indiana, besides two in Kentucky—altogether about four months of school. He learned his A B C, how to spell, read, write. And he had been with the other barefoot boys in butternut jeans learning "manners" under the school teacher, Andrew Crawford, who had them open a door, walk in, and say, "Howdy do?" Yet what he tasted of books in school was only a beginning, only made him hungry and thirsty, shook him with a wanting and a wanting of more and more of what was hidden between the covers of books.

He kept on saying, "The things I want to know are in books; my best friend is the man who'll git me a book I ain't read." He said that to Pitcher, the lawyer over at Rockport, nearly twenty miles away, one fall afternoon, when he walked from Pigeon Creek to Rockport and borrowed a book from Pitcher. Then when fodder-pulling time came a few days later, he shucked corn from early daylight till sundown along with his father and Dennis Hanks and John Hanks, but after supper he read the book till midnight, and at noon he hardly knew the taste of his cornbread because he had the book in front of him. It was a hundred little things like these which made Dennis Hanks say there was "suthin' peculiarsome" about Abe.

Besides reading the family Bible and figuring his way all through the old arithmetic they had at home, he got hold of "Æsop's Fables," "Pilgrim's Progress," "Robinson Crusoe," and Weems's "The Life of Francis Marion." The book of fables, written or collected thousands of years ago by the Greek slave, known as Æsop, sank deep in his mind. As he read through the book a second and third time, he had a feeling there were fables all around him, that everything he touched and handled, everything he saw and learned had a fable wrapped in it somewhere. One fable was about a bundle of sticks and a farmer whose sons were quarreling and fighting.

There was a fable in two sentences which read, "A coachman, hearing one of the wheels of his coach make a

"THE THINGS I WANT TO KNOW"

great noise, and perceiving that it was the worst one of the
four, asked how it came to take such a liberty. The wheel
answered that from the beginning of time, creaking had
always been the privilege of the weak." And there were
shrewd, brief incidents of foolery such as this: "A wag-
gish, idle fellow in a country town, being desirous of playing a trick on the simplicity of his neighbors and at the
same time putting a little money in his pocket at their cost,
advertised that he would on a certain day show a wheel
carriage that should be so contrived as to go without horses.
By silly curiosity the rustics were taken in, and each suc-
ceeding group who came out from the show were ashamed
to confess to their neighbors that they had seen nothing
but a wheelbarrow."

The style of the Bible, of Æsop's fables, the hearts and
minds back of those books, were much in his thoughts. His
favorite pages in them he read over and over. Behind such
proverbs as, "Muzzle not the ox that treadeth out the
corn," and "He that ruleth his own spirit is greater than
he that taketh a city," there was a music of simple wisdom
and a mystery of common everyday life that touched deep
spots in him, while out of the fables of the ancient Greek
slave he came to see that cats, rats, dogs, horses, plows,
hammers, fingers, toes, people, all had fables connected
with their lives, characters, places. There was, perhaps,

an outside for each thing as it stood alone, while inside of it was its fable.

One book came, titled, "The Life of George Washington, with Curious Anecdotes, Equally Honorable to Himself and Exemplary to His Young Countrymen. Embellished with Six Steel Engravings, by M. L. Weems, formerly Rector of Mt. Vernon Parish." It pictured men of passion and proud ignorance in the government of England driving their country into war on the American colonies. It quoted the far-visioned warning of Chatham to the British parliament, "For God's sake, then, my lords, let the way be instantly opened for reconciliation. I say instantly; or it will be too late forever."

The book told of war, as at Saratoga. "Hoarse as a mastiff of true British breed, Lord Balcarras was heard from rank to rank, loud-animating his troops; while on the other hand, fierce as a hungry Bengal tiger, the impetuous Arnold precipitated heroes on the stubborn foe. Shrill and terrible, from rank to rank, resounds the clash of bayonets —frequent and sad the groans of the dying. Pairs on pairs, Britons and Americans, with each his bayonet at his brother's breast, fall forward together faint-shrieking in death, and mingle their smoking blood." Washington, the man, stood out, as when he wrote, "These things so harassed my heart with grief, that I solemnly declared to

God, if I know myself, I would gladly offer myself a sacrifice to the butchering enemy, if I could thereby insure the safety of these my poor distressed countrymen."

The Weems book reached some deep spots in the boy. He asked himself what it meant that men should march, fight, bleed, go cold and hungry for the sake of what they called "freedom."

"Few great men are great in everything," said the book. And there was a cool sap in the passage: "His delight was in that of the manliest sort, which, by stringing the limbs and swelling the muscles, promotes the kindliest flow of blood and spirits. At jumping with a long pole, or heaving heavy weights, for his years he hardly had an equal."

Such book talk was a comfort against the same thing over again, day after day, so many mornings the same kind of water from the same spring, the same fried pork and corn-meal to eat, the same drizzles of rain, spring plowing, summer weeds, fall fodder-pulling, each coming every year, with the same tired feeling at the end of the day, so many days alone in the woods or the fields or else the same people to talk with, people from whom he had learned all they could teach him. Yet there ran through his head the stories and sayings of other people, the stories and sayings of books, the learning his eyes had caught from books; they were a comfort; they were good to have because they were good by themselves; and they were still better to have because they broke the chill of the lonesome feeling.

He was thankful to the writer of Æsop's fables because that writer stood by him and walked with him, an invisible companion, when he pulled fodder or chopped wood. Books lighted lamps in the dark rooms of his gloomy hours. . . . Well—he would live on; maybe the time would come when he would be free from work for a few weeks, or a few months, with books, and then he would read. . . . God, then he would read. . . . Then he would go and get at the proud secrets of his books.

His father—would he be like his father when he grew up? He hoped not. Why should his father knock him off a fence rail when he was asking a neighbor, passing by, a question? Even if it was a smart question, too pert and too quick, it was no way to handle a boy in front of a neighbor. No, he was going to be a man different from his father. The books—his father hated the books. His father talked about "too much eddication"; after readin', writin', 'rithmetic, that was enough, his father said. He, Abe Lincoln, the boy, wanted to know more than the father, Tom Lincoln, wanted to know. Already Abe knew more than his father; he was writing letters for the neighbors; they hunted out the Lincoln farm to get young Abe to find his bottle of ink with blackberry brier root and copperas in it, and his pen made from a turkey buzzard feather, and write letters. Abe had a suspicion sometimes his father was a little proud to have a boy that could write letters, and tell about things in books, and outrun and outwrestle and rough-and-tumble any boy or man in Spencer County. Yes, he would be different from his father; he was already so; it couldn't be helped.

In growing up from boyhood to young manhood, he had survived against lonesome, gnawing monotony and against floods, forest and prairie fires, snake-bites, horse-kicks, ague, chills, fever, malaria, "milk-sick."

A comic outline against the sky he was, hiking along the roads of Spencer and other counties in southern Indiana in those years when he read all the books within a fifty-mile circuit of his home. Stretching up on the long legs that ran from his moccasins to the body frame with its long, gangling arms, covered with linsey-woolsey, then the lean neck that carried the head with its surmounting coonskin cap or straw hat—it was, again, a comic outline —yet with a portent in its shadow. His laughing "Howdy," his yarns and drollery, opened the doors of men's hearts.

Starting along in his eleventh year came spells of abstraction. When he was spoken to, no answer came from him. "He might be a thousand miles away." The roaming, fathoming, searching, questioning operations of the minds and hearts of poets, inventors, beginners who take facts stark, these were at work in him. This was one sort of abstraction he knew; there was another: the blues took him; coils of multiplied melancholies wrapped their blue frustrations inside him, all that Hamlet, Koheleth, Schopenhauer have uttered, in a mesh of foiled hopes. "There was absolutely nothing to excite ambition for education," he wrote later of that Indiana region. Against these "blues," he found the best warfare was to find people and trade with them his yarns and drolleries. John Baldwin, the blacksmith, with many stories and odd talk and eye-slants, was a help and a light.

Days came when he sank deep in the stream of human life and felt himself kin of all that swam in it, whether the waters were crystal or mud.

He learned how suddenly life can spring a surprise. One day in the woods, as he was sharpening a wedge on a log, the ax glanced, nearly took his thumb off, and left a white scar after healing.

"You never cuss a good ax," was a saying in those timbers.

CHAPTER XIX

SIXTEEN-YEAR-OLD Abe had worked on the farm of James Taylor, at the mouth of Anderson Creek, on that great highway of traffic, the Ohio River. Besides plowing and doing barn and field work, he ran the ferryboat across the Ohio. Two travelers wanted to get on a steamboat one day, and after Abe sculled them to it and lifted their trunks on board they threw him a half-dollar apiece; it gave him a new feeling; the most he had ever earned before that was at butchering for thirty-one cents a day. And when one of the half-dollars slipped from him and sank in the river, that too gave him a new feeling.

At Anderson Creek ferry, he saw and talked with settlers, land buyers and sellers, traders, hunters, peddlers, preachers, gamblers, politicians, teachers, and men shut-mouthed about their business. Occasionally came a customer who looked as if he might be one of the "half horse, half alligator men" haunting the Ohio watercourse those years. There was river talk about Mike Fink, known on the Ohio as the "Snapping Turtle" and on the Mississippi as "The Snag," the toughest of the "half horse, half alligator" crowd; he was a famous marksman and aiming his rifle from his keel-boat floating the Ohio had shot off the tails of pigs running loose in the bottom lands.

Along the water-front of Louisville, Mike Fink had backed up his claim, "I can outrun, outhop, outjump, throw down, drag out, and lick any man in the country; I'm a Salt River roarer; I love the wimming and I'm chockfull of fight." They tried him for crimes in Louisville and acquitted him for lack of sufficient evidence; he waved a red bandanna for a good-by and told them he would come back to face their other indictments.

One of Mike's nicknames was "The Valley King." In a dispute with a man who claimed to have royal blood of France in his veins, Mike closed the argument by kicking

THE VALLEY KING

HALF HORSE, HALF ALLIGATOR MEN

the representative of royalty from the inside of a tavern to the middle of a street, with the words, "What if you are a king? Ain't we all kings over here?" His keel-boat was named "The Lightfoot." Mike's rival among the "half horse, half alligator" men was Little Billy, whose challenge ran, "I'm Little Billy, all the way from North Fork of Muddy Run and I can whip any man in this section of the country. Maybe you never heard of the time the horse kicked me an' put both his hips out o' j'int—if it ain't true, cut me up for catfish bait. I'm one o' the toughest—live forever and then turn to a white-oak post. I can outrun, outjump, outswim, chaw more tobacco and spit less, drink more whisky and keep soberer, than any man in these parts."

"Fights was fights in them days." Travelers had a proverb that a tavern was hardly safe if the proprietor had a nose or an ear off. It was a sign the landlord couldn't take care of himself.

Many travelers carried jugs of whisky, with corncob stoppers. Their common names for the raw article were such as "Red Eye," "Fire Water," "Cider Royal," "Blue Ruin," "Fool Water," "Bug Juice," though there were special brands indicative of lore and lingo with their names, "Clay and Huysen," "Race Horse," "Ching Ching," "Tog," "Rappee," "Fiscal Agent," "T. O. U.,"

"Tippena Pecco," "Moral Suasion," "Vox Populi," "Ne Plus Ultra," "Shambro," "Pig and Whistle," "Silver Top," "Poor Man's Punco," "Split Ticket," "Deacon," "Exchange," "Stone Wall," "Virginia Fence," "Floater," and "Shifter."

In Louisville, men played billiards all night, and there were no closing hours for the saloons and poker-rooms; a legend ran of one gambler dealing the cards when alarm was sounded that a steamboat at the river landing was on fire, and he went on asking the players, "How many?" as though steamboats caught fire every day. The Hope Distillery Company, capitalized at $100,000, was operating with grain from the near-by Kentucky and Scioto River valleys, while one Dr. McMurtrie called the Hope concern "a gigantic reservoir of damning drink; they manufacture poison for the human race; of what avail are the reasonings of philanthropists?"

So risky was travel that the Indiana legislature specifically permitted travelers to carry concealed weapons of any kind. There were traders from Cincinnati to New Orleans who were familiar with a regular dialogue, which they rehearsed to each other when they had the same room or bed in a tavern. "Stranger," one would say, "it's been a mighty long time since you and me slep' together." "Yep," came the regulation answer. "Got the same old smell you

used to have?" "You *bet*." "Air you as lousy as ever?"
"That's me." "Put 'er thar!" Then with a handshake and
a swig from the jug they went to their sleep. There were

tales of mosquitoes of a certain breed along the Ohio
River; two could kill a dog, ten a man.

Men who had made trips up and down the river more
than once had a song with a chorus:

> Hard upon the beach oar!
>   She moves too slow.
> All the way to Shawneetown,
>   Long time ago.

A song, "The Hunters of Kentucky," written by Samuel Woodworth, the author of "The Old Oaken Bucket," was heard occasionally amid the Ohio River traffic. It was about the Kentuckians at the Battle of New Orleans; a force of 2,250 of them had marched overland, arriving half-naked; women of New Orleans cut and sewed 1,127 "pairs of pantaloons" for them from wool blankets, in less than five days. Part of the song ran:

> And if a daring foe annoys,
>   No matter what his force is,
> We'll show him that Kentucky boys
>   Are alligator-horses.

After telling about the breastworks erected for the battle, the song had this to say:

> Behind it stood our little force,
>   None wished it to be greater,
> For every man was half a horse
>   And half an alligator.

Lawyers with books in their saddlebags took the ferryboat across the Ohio; law and order was coming to that wild young country, they believed; they could remember only ten years back how the law of the Territory of Indiana provided that a horse-thief should have two hundred lashes with a whip on his bare back and stay in jail till the horse was paid for, and the second time he was caught horse-stealing he was shot or hanged; for stealing cattle or hogs the thief had his shirt taken off and was given thirty-nine lashes.

Hunters crossed Anderson Creek ferry who could tell how George Doty in 1821 up in Johnson County killed 300 deer. They said Noah Major, one of the first settlers in Morgan County, estimated there were 20,000 deer in that county when he came in 1820, six years before. Circuit riders could tell about Peter Cartwright, who twenty years before was riding the Salt River district in Kentucky, occasionally getting over into Indiana; once Cartwright labored with a community of Shakers till eighty-seven of that sect were "rescued from the delusion." Those circuit riders could tell about Samuel Thornton Scott, the Presbyterian wilderness preacher, who swam the White River, losing his hat and one boot, arriving at Vincennes, as one friend said, "neither naked nor clad, barefoot nor shod."

Old-timers came along who could tell how the Indians in 1809 were stealing horses, burning barns and fences, killing settlers, running off with cattle and chickens, and how General Hopkins with 1,200 soldiers burned the Indian villages along the Wabash, their log cabins, gardens, orchards, stationed rangers to hunt down every Indian they found, till the time came when there was not a red man on the Wabash or south of that river in the state of Indiana.

Others could tell of Daniel Ketcham, who was taken by Indians, kept over winter near Madison, loaded like a mule and marched to one of the Miami rivers, where his skin was blacked and he was handed a looking-glass and told to have a last look at himself before burning at the stake. A daughter of the chief, wearing five hundred silver brooches, made a thirty-minute speech, words flying fast and with defiance. Then she let Ketcham loose, two Indian women washed the black off him "and the white blood out"; he was taken to the tent of their mother, who offered him her hand but, being drunk, fell off her seat before he could take the hand. He carried wood, pounded corn, escaped and returned home to his wife, who had pledged neighbors that Ketcham, who was a famous wheat-stacker, would be home in time for stacking that year.

The ferry boy at Anderson Creek watched and listened to this human drift across the Ohio River, the bushwhackers and bad men who called themselves bad, and the others who called themselves good. Civilization went by, boats and tools breaking ways. Steamboats came past in a slow and proud pageantry making their fourteen- to twenty-day passage from New Orleans to Pittsburgh; geography became fact to the boy looking on; the flags on the steam-

boats were a sign of that long stretch of country the steamboats were crossing. Strings of flatboats passed, loaded with
produce, pork, turkeys, chicken, cornmeal, flour, whisky,
venison hams, hazel-nuts, skins, furs, ginseng; this was
farm produce for trading at river ports to merchants or
to plantation owners for feeding slaves. Other trading
boats carried furniture, groceries, clothes, kitchenware,
plows, wagons, harness; this was from manufacturing
centers, consignments to storekeepers and traders. House-
boats, arks, sleds, flatboats with small cabins in which
families lived and kept house, floated toward their new
homesteads; on these the women were washing, the children playing. The life-flow of a main artery of American
civilization, at a vivid line of growth, was a piece of pageantry there at Anderson Creek.

CHAPTER XX

YOUNG Abe was out with ax, saw, and draw-knife building himself a light flatboat at Bates's Landing, a mile and a half down the river from Anderson's Creek. He was eighteen years old, a designer, builder, navigator; he cut down trees, hewed out planks, pegged and cleated together the bottoms and sides of his own boat, wood from end to end.

Pieces of money jingled in his pockets. Passengers paid him for sculling them from Bates's Landing out to steamboats in the middle of the Ohio River.

He studied words and figurations on pieces of money. Thirteen stars stood for the first Thirteen States of the Union. The silver print of an eagle spreading its wings and lifting a fighting head was on the half-dollar. As though the eagle were crying high, important words, above its beak was inscribed "E Pluribus Unum"; this meant the many states should be One, young Abe learned.

Circled with the thirteen stars were the head and bust of a motherly-looking woman. On her forehead was the word "Liberty." Just what did *She* mean?

Waiting for passengers and looking out on the wide Ohio to the drooping trees that dipped their leaves in the water on the farther shore, he could think about money and women and eagles.

A signal came from the opposite shore one day and Lincoln rowed across the river. As he stepped out of his boat two men jumped out of the brush. They took hold of him and said they were going to "duck" him in the river. They were John and Lin Dill, brothers who operated a ferry and claimed Abe had been transporting passengers for hire contrary to the law of Kentucky.

As they sized up Abe's lean husky arms they decided not to throw him in the river. He might be too tough a customer. Then all three went to Squire Samuel Pate, justice of the peace, near Lewisport.

A warrant for the arrest of Abraham Lincoln was sworn out by John T. Dill. And the trial began of the case of "The Commonwealth of Kentucky versus Abraham Lincoln," charged with violation of "An Act Respecting the Establishment of Ferries."

Lincoln testified he had carried passengers from the Indiana shore out to the middle of the river, never taking them to the Kentucky shore. And the Dill brothers, though sore and claiming the defendant Lincoln had wronged them, did not go so far as to testify he had "for reward set any person over a river," in the words of the Kentucky statute.

Squire Pate dismissed the warrant against Lincoln. The disappointed Dills put on their hats and left. Lincoln sat with Squire Pate for a long talk. If a man knows the law about a business he is in, it is a help to him, the Squire told young Abe.

They shook hands and parted friends. Afterwards on days when no passengers were in sight and it was "law day" at Squire Pate's down the river, Abe would scull over and watch the witnesses, the constables, the Squire, the machinery of law, government, justice.

The State of Indiana, he learned, was one thing, and the State of Kentucky, something else. A water line in the middle of a big river ran between them. He could ask: "Who makes state lines? What *are* state lines?"

CHAPTER XXI

IN the year 1825, ox teams and pack horses came through Gentryville carrying people on their way to a place on the Wabash River they called New Harmony. A rich English business man named Robert Owen had paid $132,000.00 for land and $50,000.00 for live stock, tools, and merchandise, and had made a speech before the Congress at Washington telling how he and his companions were going to try to find a new way for people to live their lives together, without fighting, cheating, or exploiting each other, where work would be honorable yet there would be time for play and learning; they would share and share alike, each for all and all for each. In January, 1826, Owen himself, with a party of 30 people came down the Ohio River in what was called the "boatload of knowledge."

More ox wagons and pack horses kept coming past the Gentryville crossroads; about a thousand people were joined in Owen's scheme at New Harmony on the Wabash. The scheme lighted up Abe Lincoln's heart. His eyes were big and hungry as a hoot-owl's as he told Dennis Hanks, "There's a school and thousands of books there and fellers that know everything in creation." The schooling would have cost him about $100 a year and he could have worked for his board. But Tom Lincoln had other plans for his son Abe.

Across the next three years the boy grew longer of leg and arm, tougher of bone and sinew, with harder knuckles and joints. James Gentry, with the largest farms in the Pigeon Creek clearings, and a landing on the Ohio River, was looking the big boy over. He believed Abe could take his pork, flour, meal, bacon, potatoes, and produce to trade down the Mississippi River, for cotton, tobacco, and sugar. Young Abe was set to work on a flatboat; he cut the oaks for a double bottom of stout planks, and a deck shelter, two pairs of long oars at bow and stern, a check-post, and a setting pole for steering.

As the snow and ice began to melt, a little before the first frogs started shrilling, in that year of 1828, they loaded the boat and pushed off.

In charge of the boat Mr. Gentry had placed his son Allen, and in charge of Allen he had placed Abe Lincoln, to hold his own against any half horse, half alligator bushwhackers who might try to take the boat or loot it, and leave the bones of those they took it from, at Cave-in-Rock on the Illinois shore, or other spots where the skeletons of flatboatmen had been found years after the looters sold the cargo down the river. The honesty of Abe, of course, had been the first point Mr. Gentry considered; and the next point had been whether he could handle the boat in the snags and sand-bars. The two young men pushed off on their trip of a thousand miles to New Orleans, on a wide, winding waterway, where the flatboats were tied up at night to the river-bank, and floated and poled by day amid changing currents, strings of other flatboats, and in the paths of the proud white steamboats.

Whitecaps rose and broke with their foam feathers, a mile, two miles, beyond the limit of eyesight, as fresh winds blew along the Ohio River. Cave-in-Rock was

[163]

passed on the Illinois shore, with its sign, "Wilson's Liquor Vault and House of Entertainment," with a doorway 25 feet high, 80 feet wide, and back of that entrance a cavern 200 feet deep, a 14-foot chimney leading to an upper room, where one time later were found 60 human skeletons, most of them rivermen lured and trapped by the Wilson gang that camped at Hurricane Island near by.

Timber-covered river bluffs stood up overlooking the river like plowmen resting big shoulders between the plowhandles; twisted dumps and runs of clay banks were like squatters who had lost hope and found rheumatism and malaria; lone pine trees had silhouetted their dry arms of branches on reefs where they dissolved and reappeared in river-mist lights as if they struggled to tell some secret of water and sky before going under.

The nineteen-year-old husky from Indiana found the Mississippi River as tricky with comic twists as Æsop's fables, as mystical, boding, and promising as the family Bible. Sand-bars, shoals, and islands were scattered along with the look of arithmetic numbers. Sudden rains, shifting winds, meant new handling of oars. A rising roar and rumble of noise might be rough water ahead or some whimsical current tearing through fallen tree-branches at the river side. A black form seems to be floating up-river through a gray drizzle; the coming out of the sun shows

ON THE MISSISSIPPI

it is an island point, standing still; the light and air play tricks with it.

The bends of the river ahead must be watched with ready oars and sweeps or the flatboat naturally heads in to shore. Strong winds crook the course of the boat, sometimes blowing it ashore; one of the crew must hustle off in a rowboat, tie a hawser to a tree or stump, while another man on the big boat has a rope at the check-post; and they slow her down. Warning signals must be given at night, by waving lantern or firewood, to other craft.

So the flatboat, "the broadhorn," went down the Father of Waters, four to six miles an hour, the crew frying their own pork and corn-meal cakes, washing their own shirts, sewing on their own buttons.

Below Baton Rouge, among the sugar plantations known as the "Sugar Coast," they tied up at the plantation of Madame Duquesne one evening, put their boat in order, spoke their good nights to any sweet stars in the sky, and dropped off to sleep. They woke to find seven negroes on board trying to steal the cargo and kill the crew; the long-armed Indiana husky swung a crab-tree club, knocked them galley-west, chased them into the woods, and came back to the boat and laid a bandanna on a gash over the right eye that left a scar for life as it healed. Then they cut loose the boat and moved down the river.

[167]

At New Orleans they traded, sold the rest of their cargo of potatoes, bacon, hams, flour, apples, jeans, in exchange for cotton, tobacco, and sugar, and sold the flatboat for what it would bring as lumber. And they lingered and loitered a few days, seeing New Orleans, before taking steamer north.

On the streets and by-streets of that town, which had floated the flags of French, British, and American dominion, young Abraham Lincoln felt the pulses of a living humanity with far heartbeats in wide, alien circles over the earth: English sailors who sang "Ranzo" and "Boney," "Hangin' Johnny," and "O Fare-you-well, My Bonny Young Girls"; Dutchmen and French in jabber and exclamative; Swedes, Norwegians, and Russians with blond and reddish mustaches and whiskers; Spaniards and Italians with knives and red silk handkerchiefs; New York, Philadelphia, Boston, Rome, Amsterdam, become human facts; it was London those men came from, ejaculating, " 'Ow can ye blime me?"

Women in summer weather wearing slippers and boots; creoles with dusks of eyes; quadroons and octoroons with elusive soft voices; streets lined with saloons where men drank with men or chose from the women sipping their French wine or Jamaica rum at tables, sending quiet signals with their eyes or openly slanging the sailors, team-

NEW ORLEANS

sters, roustabouts, rivermen, timber cruisers, crap-shooters, poker sharps, squatters, horse thieves, poor whites; bets were laid on steamboat races; talk ran fast about the construction, then going on, of the New Orleans & Pontchartrain Railroad, to be one of the first steam railroads in America and the world; slaves passed handcuffed into gangs headed for cotton fields of one, two, six thousand acres in size; and everywhere was talk about niggers, good and bad niggers, how to rawhide the bad ones with mule whips or bring 'em to N' Orleans and sell 'em; and how you could trust your own children with a good nigger.

As young Abe Lincoln and Allen Gentry made their way back home to the clearings of Pigeon Creek, Indiana, the tall boy had his thoughts. He had crossed half the United States, it seemed, and was back home after three months' vacation with eight dollars a month pay in his pocket and a scar over the right eye.

That year Indiana University was to print its first catalogue, but Abe Lincoln didn't show up among the students who registered. He was between the plow handles or pulling fodder or sinking the ax in trees and brush, and reading between times "Pilgrim's Progress," a history of the United States, the life of Francis Marion, the life of Ben Franklin, and the book he borrowed from Dave Turnham, the constable. The title-page of the book said it con-

tained, "The Revised Laws of Indiana, adopted and en-
acted by the general assembly at their eighth session. To
which are prefixed the Declaration of Independence, the
Constitution of the United States, the Constitution of the
State of Indiana, and sundry other documents connected
with the Political History of the Territory and State of
Indiana. Arranged and published by the authority of the
General Assembly."

The science of government, theories of law, and schemes
of administration spread themselves before the young
man's mind as he crept along from page to page, wrestling
with those statutes of Indiana and other documents. It was
tough plowing through that book, with the satisfaction,
however, that he could keep what he earned. Crimes and
punishments were listed there, in black and white, fine dis-
tinctions between murder and manslaughter, between bur-
glary, robbery, larceny, forgery, trespass, nuisance, fraud;
varied circumstances of assault and battery, affray, unlaw-
ful assembly, rout and riot.

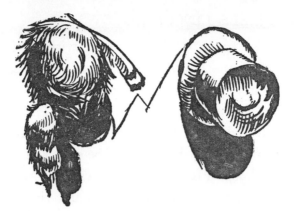

CHAPTER XXII

READING the *Louisville Gazette* which came weekly to Gentryville, working out as chore-boy, field-hand and ferryman, walking a fifty-mile circuit around the home cabin, flatboating down the Ohio and Mississippi, the young man Abraham Lincoln took in many things with his eyes that saw and his ears that heard and remembered. A Virginia planter named Edward Coles had quit Virginia and come down the Ohio River with his slaves, ending his journey in Illinois, where he had deeded a farm to each of his slaves with papers of freedom. The Erie Canal in New York, a big ditch for big boats to run on, was finished; it cost seven and a half million dollars but it connected the Great Lakes and the Atlantic Ocean and it meant that the north ends of Indiana and Illinois, besides other prairie stretches, were going to fill up faster with settlers. The first railroad in the United States, a stub line three miles long, was running iron-wheeled wagons on iron rails at Quincy, Massachusetts. A settlement called Indianapolis had been cleared away. Glass and nails were arriving in southern Indiana now; there used to be none at all ten years back. The famous Frenchman, General LaFayette, came up the Mississippi from New Orleans and visited Kaskaskia, where a reception was held in a mansion with the windows kept open for the benefit of people outside who wanted to have a look in. Sam Patch, who slid down Niagara Falls once, and lived, had slid down the Genesee Falls at Rochester, New York, and was killed.

It was interesting that Henry Clay, the famous congressman and orator from Kentucky, was nicknamed "The Mill Boy of the Slashes," and came from a family of poor farmers and used to ride to mill with a sack of corn. It was interesting to hear a story that Henry Clay's wife was asked by a Boston woman in Washington, "Doesn't it distress you to have Mr. Clay gambling with cards?" and that she answered, "Oh, dear, no! He most always wins."

Fragments of talk and newspaper items came about Daniel Webster, and his Bunker Hill speech at the cornerstone of the Bunker Hill monument, or John Marshall, Chief Justice of the Supreme Court, and a decision in law, but they were far off. There was a sharp-tongued senator from Virginia, John Randolph of Roanoke, who was bitter against John Calhoun, vice president of the United States; and John Randolph one day pointed his finger at Calhoun and said: "Mr. Speaker! I mean Mr. President of the Senate and would-be President of the United States, which God in His infinite mercy avert." And Randolph during a hot speech would call to a doorkeeper, "Tims, more porter," taking every ten or fifteen minutes a foaming tumbler of malt liquor, drinking two or three quarts during a long speech.

And neither Calhoun nor anybody else interfered with John Randolph when, on the floor of the Senate, he called John Quincy Adams, the President of the United States, "a traitor," or Daniel Webster "a vile slanderer," or Edward Livingston "the most contemptible and degraded of beings, whom no man ought to touch, unless with a pair of tongs." In some stories about famous men there seemed to be a touch of the comic; John Randolph on the Senate floor called Henry Clay a "blackleg"; they fought a duel with pistols; Clay shot Randolph twice in the pantaloons; Randolph shot off his pistol once "accidentally" and once in the air; both sides came through alive and satisfied.

Southern and western congressmen kept dueling pistols in their Washington outfits; some had special pistols inlaid with gold. A Philadelphia gunsmith named Derringer was winning popularity with a short pistol to be carried in the hip pocket and used in street fights. At the "exclusive" assembly balls in Washington, the women's skirts came down to slightly above the ankles; their silk stockings were embroidered with figures called "clocks" and their thin slippers had silk rosettes and tiny silver buckles. The fashionable men of "exclusive" society affairs wore frock coats of blue, green, or claret cloth, with gilt buttons; shirts were of ruffled linen; they had baggy "Cossack" pantaloons tucked into "Hessian" boots with gold top tassels.

Everybody in the capital knew that the justices of the Supreme Court took snuff from their snuffboxes while hearing causes argued; that Henry Clay was moderate about drinking whisky, while Daniel Webster went too far; that Andrew Jackson smoked a corn-cob pipe, and his enemies were free to say Mrs. Jackson too enjoyed her daily pipe. Protests were made to the Government against the transportation of the mails on Sunday; in Philadelphia church people stretched chains fastened with padlocks across the streets to stop the passage of mail-coaches.

The stories drifted west about white men in New York City who held political processions in which they marched dressed like Indians; they had organized the Tammany

Society back in 1789; the members died but Tammany lived on. The big excitement of New York politics had been the struggle of De Witt Clinton, the governor, to put through the digging of the Erie Canal, against Tammany opposition.

> Oh, a ditch he would dig from the lakes to the sea.
> The Eighth of the world's matchless Wonders to be.
> Good land! How absurd! But why should you grin?
> It will do to bury its mad author in.

So Tammany sang at the start. But De Witt Clinton stuck with the tenacity of his forefathers who had fought against the Indians and against the British king. When he won out, the rhymes ran:

> Witt Clinton is dead, St. Tammany said,
> And all the papooses with laughter were weeping;
> But Clinton arose and confounded his foes—
> The cunning old fox had only been sleeping.

There had been the four years John Quincy Adams was President. He had been elected in a three-cornered fight that ended on election day with Andrew Jackson having the most votes cast for him but not a majority. This had put the contest into Congress, where Henry Clay had thrown his forces to Adams; and Adams's first move was to appoint Clay Secretary of State. The Jackson men said it was a crooked deal. Jackson had handed in his resignation as Senator from Tennessee and started work on his political fences for 1828, while his New York Tammany friend, Martin Van Buren, was booming him up North. All the four years Adams was President, the moves in Congress were aimed at bagging the Presidency in 1828. Investigating committees worked overtime; each side dug for the other's scandals: Adams's past personal record; Jackson's handling of six deserters at Mobile in 1815, when 1,500 soldiers were drawn up at parade rest to watch thirty-six riflemen fire at six blindfolded men, each man kneeling on his own coffin; Adams's bills for wall paper and paint in renovating the White House; Jackson's alleged marriage to his wife before she was properly divorced.

In the background of all the bitter personal feelings, the slander and the slack talk of politics, a deep, significant drift and shift was going on. Part of it was the feeling of the West and Southwest, the raw and new country, against the East and New England, the settled and established country. Added to this was a feeling that Jackson stood for the rough, plain people who work, as against the people who don't. That was the issue, as the Jackson crowd presented it, so that even Abe Lincoln in Spencer County,

Indiana, was caught in the drive of its enthusiasm, and wrote:

> Let auld acquaintance be forgot
> And never brought to mind;
> May Jackson be our President,
> And Adams left behind.

Jackson rode to election on a tumultuous landslide of ballots. His wife, Rachel, said, "Well, for Mr. Jackson's sake, I am glad, but for my own part I never wished it." And the home women of Nashville secretly got ready dresses of satin and silk for her to wear in Washington as the first lady of the land; then death took her suddenly; her husband for hours refused to believe she had breathed her last; he had killed one man and silenced others who had spoken against her. One woman wrote, "General Jackson was never quite the same man afterward; her death subdued his spirit and corrected his speech."

Then the new President-elect sailed down the Cumberland River to the Ohio, stopped at Cincinnati and Pittsburgh, and went on to Washington for an inauguration before a crowd of ten thousand people, whose wild cheering of their hero showed they believed something new and different had arrived in the government of the American republic. Daniel Webster, writing a letter to a friend, hit off the event by saying: "I never saw such a crowd. People have come five hundred miles to see General Jackson, and they really seem to think the country is rescued from some dreadful danger." The buckskin shirts of Kentucky settlers and the moccasins of Indian fighters from Tennessee were seen in the crowd, and along with politicians, preachers, merchants, gamblers, and lookers-on, swarmed in to the White House reception, took their turns at barrels of whisky, broke punch-bowls of glass and chinaware, emptied pails of punch, stood on the satin-covered chairs and had their look at "Andy Jackson, Our President," who was shoved into a corner where a line of friends formed a barrier to protect the sixty-two-year-old man from his young buck henchmen.

Thus began an eight-year period in which Andrew Jackson was President of the United States. He came to the White House with the mud of all America's great rivers and swamps on his boots, with records of victories in battles against savage Indian tribes and trained Continental European generals who had fought Napoleon, with shattered ribs and the bullets of Tennessee duelists and gun-fighters of the Southwest in his body; he knew little grammar and many scars, few classics and many fast horses.

Jackson came taking the place of John Quincy Adams, who was asking large funds for a national university and a

JACKSON'S MEN

colossal astronomical observatory, "a lighthouse of the skies," a lovable, decent man who knew all the capes, peninsulas, and inlets of New England, who had been across the Atlantic and stood by the Thames and the Seine rivers, and had never laid eyes on the Mississippi nor the Wabash River. Harvard went under as against the Smoky Mountains and Horseshoe Bend. Jackson came in with 178 electoral votes as against 83 for Adams, after national circulation by his enemies of a thick pamphlet entitled, "Reminiscences; or an Extract from the Catalogue of General Jackson's Youthful Indiscretions, between the Age of Twenty-Three and Sixty," reciting fourteen fights, duels, brawls, shooting and cutting affairs, in which it was alleged he had killed, slashed, and clawed various American citizens. It was told of him that he asked a friend the day after the inaugural what the people were saying of his first message. "They say it is first-rate, but nobody believes you wrote it," was the answer. To which Jackson rejoined, "Well, don't I deserve just as much credit for picking out the man who could write it?"

One nickname for him was "Old Hickory"; he had lived on acorns and slept in the rain; now he sat in a second-story room of the White House smoking a cob pipe, running the United States Government as he had run his armies, his political campaigns, his Tennessee plantation,

[183]

his stable of racing horses, with a warm heart, a cool head, a sharp tongue, recklessly, cunningly; he was simple as an ax-handle, shrewd as an Indian ambush, mingling in his breast the paradoxes of the good and evil proverbs of the people.

Jackson was the son of a north-of-Irelander who came to America with only a pair of hands. "No man will ever be quite able to comprehend Andrew Jackson who has not personally known a Scotch-Irishman." His breed broke with their bare hands into the wilderness beyond the Allegheny Mountains, and more than any other one stock of blood is credited with putting the western and southwestern stretches of territory under the dominion of the central federal government at Washington. The mellowed and practiced philosopher, Thomas Jefferson, once wrote a letter with the passage, "When I was president of the Senate, he (Jackson) was a senator, and he could never speak on account of the rashness of his feelings. I have seen him attempt it repeatedly and as often choke with rage." And yet, unless the Jackson breed of men, even their extreme type, "the half horse, half alligator men," had pushed with their covered wagons, their axes and rifles, out into the territory of the Louisiana Purchase, Jefferson would have had no basis nor data for his negotiations in that mammoth land deal. Though in the presence of the ruffled linen of the Senate Jackson did "choke with rage," he faced Creek Indians, or seasoned troops from Napoleonic campaigns, or mutineers of his own army, with a cool and controlled behavior that was beyond the range of comprehension of models of etiquette in Washington.

With Jackson in the White House came a new politics, better and worse. The ax of dismissal fell on two thousand postmasters, department heads and clerks. An Administration daily newspaper, the *Washington Globe,* began publication; all office-holders earning more than one thousand dollars a year had to subscribe or lose their jobs. The editor was asked to soften an attack on an Administration enemy, and replied, "No, let it tear his heart out." Wives of Cabinet members refused to mix socially with Peggy O'Neill; talk ran that she was "fast" and of too shady a past even though now married to the Secretary of War. As the scandal dragged on, Jackson wrote hundreds of letters in her defense, sometimes using the phrase that she was "chaste as snow"; the husbands of the offended Cabinet members' wives resigned from the Cabinet; Jackson knocked the ashes from his cob pipe, appointed fresh and willing Cabinet members, and life went on as before.

When his postmaster-general, a tried and loyal friend, rebelled at making the wholesale dismissals required by the politicians, Jackson pushed him to a seat on the Supreme

Court bench, and appointed a more willing post-office chief. One friend said he was an actor, that after storming at a caller, and closing the door, he would chuckle over his pipe and say, "He thought I was mad." A mail-coach

robber, condemned to be hanged, reminded the President that once at a horse-race near Nashville he had told General Jackson to change his bets from a horse whose jockey had been "fixed" to lose the race; the death sentence was commuted to ten years in prison. "Ask nothing but what is right, submit to nothing wrong," was his advice on policies with European countries. He was well thought of by millions who believed there was truth lurking behind his

[186]

sentiment, "True virtue cannot exist where pomp and parade are the governing passions; it can only dwell with the people—the great laboring and producing classes that form the bone and sinew of our confederacy." He was alluded to as "the Tennessee Barbarian" or "King Andrew the First" in certain circles, yet the doormats of the White House got acquainted with the shoes, boots, and moccasins of a wider range of humanity as he ran the Federal Government during those first years of the eight in which he was to be President.

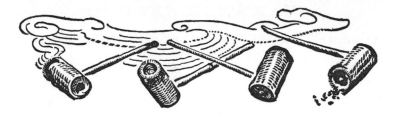

CHAPTER XXIII

ALL the way down the Mississippi to the Gulf and back, Abe Lincoln had heard about Andrew Jackson in that year of 1828 when Jackson swept that country with a big land-slide. In the newspapers that came to the post office at Gentryville, in the talk around Jones's store, in the fields harvesting, and at meetings, Andrew Jackson was the man talked about. With Andrew Jackson for President, the plainest kind of people could go into the White House and feel at home; with that kind of man, who smoked a cob pipe, talked horse sense, and rode reckless horses, and who had whipped the British at New Orleans, the Government would be more like what was meant in the Declaration of Independence and the Fourth of July speeches. Thus the talk ran.

Young Abe Lincoln heard it. The personality and the ways of Andrew Jackson filled his thoughts. He asked himself many questions and puzzled his head about the magic of this one strong, stormy man filling the history of that year, commanding a wild love from many people, and calling out curses and disgust from others, but those others were very few in Indiana. The riddles that attach to a towering and magnetic personality staged before a great public, with no very definite issues or policies in question, but with some important theory of government and art of life apparently involved behind the personality—these met young Abe's eyes and ears.

It was the year he wrote in the front cover of "The Columbian Class Book" the inscription, "Abe Lincoln 1828." The preface of the book said it contained "pieces calculated to interest the attention of the scholar and impress the mind with a knowledge of useful facts." And he borrowed from Josiah Crawford "The Kentucky Preceptor," the preface of that book saying, "Tales of love, or romantic fiction, or anything which might tend to instil false notions into the minds of children have not gained admission." There were essays on Magnanimity, Remorse of Conscience, Columbus, Demosthenes, On the Scriptures as a Rule of Life, the speech of Robert Emmet on why the English government should not hang an Irish patriot, stories of Indians, and the inaugural address of President Jefferson twenty-four years previous to that year. Jefferson spoke of "the agonizing spasms of infuriated man, seeking through blood and slaughter his long-lost liberty" in the French Revolution. Let America remember that free speech, and respect for the opinions of others, are measures of safety, was the advice of Jefferson.

Then Abe Lincoln read the passage from the pen of Jefferson: "If there be any among us who would wish to dissolve this Union, or to change its republican form, let them stand as monuments of the safety with which error of opinion may be tolerated where reason is left free to combat it. I know, indeed, that some honest men fear a republican government cannot be strong, that this government is not strong enough. . . . I believe this, on the contrary, the strongest government on earth."

Young nineteen-year-old Abe Lincoln had plenty to think about in that year of 1828, what with his long trip to New Orleans and back, what with the strong, stormy Andrew Jackson sweeping into control of the Government at Washington, and the gentle, teasing, thoughtful words of Thomas Jefferson: "Sometimes it is said that man cannot be trusted with the government of himself. Can he then be trusted with the government of others?"

CHAPTER XXIV

For more than twenty years Johnny Appleseed had been making his name one to laugh at and love in the log cabins between the Ohio River and the northern lakes. In 1806, he loaded two canoes with apple seeds at cider mills in western Pennsylvania and floated down the Ohio River to the Muskingum, along which he curved to White Woman Creek, the Mohican, the Black Fork, making a long stay on the borders of Licking Creek and in Licking County, where many farmers were already thanking him for their orchards. As he ran out of seeds he rode a bony horse or walked back to western Pennsylvania to fill two leather bags with apple seeds at cider mills; then in the

Ohio territory where he tramped, he would pick out loamy land, plant the seeds, pile brush around, and tell the farmers to help themselves from the young shoots. He went barefoot till winter came, and was often seen in late November walking in mud and snow. Neither snakes, Indians nor foreign enemies had harmed him. Children had seen him stick pins and needles into his tough flesh; when he sat at a table with a farmer family he wouldn't eat till he was sure there was plenty for the children. Asked if he wasn't afraid of snakes as he walked barefoot in the brush, he pulled a New Testament from his pocket and said, "This book is protection against all danger here and hereafter." When taken in overnight by a farmer, he would ask if they wanted to hear "some news right fresh from heaven," and then stretch out on the floor and read, "Blessed are the meek, for they shall inherit the earth" and other Beatitudes. A woman said of his voice that it was "loud as the roar of wind and waves, then soft and soothing as the balmy airs that quivered the morning-glory leaves about his gray beard."

Once the camp-fire of Johnny Appleseed drew many mosquitoes which were burning; he quenched the fire, explaining to friends, "God forbid that I should build a fire for my comfort which should be the means of destroying any of His creatures!" During most of the year he wore

JOHNNY APPLESEED

no clothes except for a coffee sack with armholes cut in it; and a stump preacher once near the village of Mansfield was crying, "Where now is there a man who, like the primitive Christians, is traveling to Heaven barefooted and clad in coarse raiment?" when Johnny Appleseed came forward to put a bare foot on the pulpit stump and declare, "Here's your primitive Christian." A hornet stung him and he plucked out the hornet from a wrinkle of the coffee sack and let it go free. He claimed that his religion brought him into conversations with angels; two of the angels with whom he talked were to be his wives in heaven provided he never married on earth. What little money he needed came from farmers willing to pay for young apple trees. As settlements and villages came thicker, he moved west with the frontier, planting apple seeds, leaving trails of orchards in his paths over a territory of a hundred thousand square miles in Ohio and Indiana.

These were the years John James Audubon, who had kept a store in Elizabethtown, Kentucky, was traveling the Ohio and Mississippi River regions, with knapsack, dog, and gun, hunting birds, to paint them in oil on canvas "with their own lively animated ways when seeking their natural food and pleasure." He was among pioneers who moved from Kentucky and settled at Princeton, Indiana, a walker who walked on thousand-mile trips, leaving his

[195]

wife to stay with friends while he lived with wild birds and shot them and sketched their forms.

Audubon's notebook told of canoeing in flood-swollen Mississippi river-bottom lands. "All is silent and melancholy, unless when the mournful bleating of the hemmed-in deer reaches your ear, or the dismal scream of an eagle

or a heron is heard, or the foul bird rises, disturbed by your approach, from the carcass on which it was allaying its craving appetite. Bears, cougars, lynxes, and all other quadrupeds that can ascend the trees, are observed crouched among their top branches; hungry in the midst of abundance, although they see floating around them the animals on which they usually prey. They dare not venture to swim

[196]

to them. Fatigued by the exertions which they have made in reaching dry land, they will there stand near the hunter's fire, as if to die by a ball were better than to perish amid the waste of waters. On occasions like this, all these animals are shot by hundreds."

Audubon went East to Philadelphia in 1824, gave an exhibition of his paintings, sold less than enough to pay for the show, and was told not to publish his work. In 1827 he began his issues of a work titled "The Birds of America," which when finished was in eighty-seven parts. That same year he reached London, where a barber cut off the ringlets of hair falling to his shoulders, and he wrote, under date of March 19, 1827, "This day my hair was sacrificed, and the will of God usurped by the wishes of Man. My heart sank low." He became an international authority, and sat up till half-past three one morning writing a paper to be read the next day before the Natural History Society of London on the habits of the wild pigeon. "So absorbed was my whole soul and spirit in the work, that I felt as if I were in the woods of America among the pigeons, and my ears filled with the sound of their rustling wings."

After reading his paper before the society, Audubon wrote the commentary: "Captain Hall expressed some doubts as to my views respecting the affection and love of pigeons, as if I made it human, and raised the possessors quite above the brutes. I presume the love of the (pigeon) mothers for their young is much the same as the love of woman for her offspring. There is but one kind of love: God is love, and all his creatures derive theirs from his; only it is modified by the different degrees of intelligence in different beings and creatures."

Thus Audubon, who had sold Sunday clothes to his customers in Elizabethtown, Kentucky. He and Abe Lincoln had footed the same red clay highways of Hardin County, floated the same Ohio and Mississippi rivers, fought in the night against other forms of life that came to kill. Both loved birds and people. Each was a child of hope.

CHAPTER XXV

In the fall of 1829, Abraham Lincoln was putting his ax
to big trees and whipsawing logs into planks for lumber
to build a house on his father's farm. But his father made
new plans; the lumber was sold to Josiah Crawford; and
the obedient young axman was put to work cutting and
sawing trees big enough around to make wagon-wheels,
and hickories tough enough for axles and poles on an ox-
wagon.

The new plans were that the Lincoln family and the

families of Dennis Hanks and Levi Hall, married to Abe's step-sisters, thirteen people in all, were going to move to Macon County over in Illinois, into a country with a river the Indians named Sangamo, meaning "the land of plenty to eat." The Lincoln farm wasn't paying well; after buying eighty acres for $2.00 an acre and improving it for fourteen years, Tom Lincoln sold it to Charles Grigsby for $125.00 cash before signing the papers.

The milk-sick was taking farm animals; since Dennis Hanks lost four milk-cows and eleven calves in one week, besides having a spell of the sickness himself, Dennis was saying, "I'm goin' t' git out o' here and hunt a country where the milk-sick is not; it's like to ruined me."

In September Tom Lincoln and his wife had made a trip down to Elizabethtown, Kentucky, where they sold for $123.00 the lot which Mrs. Lincoln had fallen heir to when her first husband died; the clerk, Samuel Haycraft, filled out the deed of sale, declaring that she "was examined by me privately and apart from her said husband" and did "freely and willingly subscribe to the sale." And Tom, with the cash from this sale and the money from the sale of his own farm, was buying oxen, or young steers, and trading and selling off household goods.

Moving was natural to his blood; he came from a long line of movers; he could tell about the family that had

PUTTING HIS AX TO BIG TREES

moved so often that their chickens knew the signs of another moving; and the chickens would walk up to the
mover, stretch flat on the ground, and put up their feet to
be tied for the next wagon trip.

The men-folks that winter, using their broadaxes and
draw-knives on solid blocks of wood, shaping wagon
wheels, had a church scandal to talk about. Tom Lincoln
and his wife had been granted by the Pigeon church a
"letter of Dismission," to show they had kept up their
obligations and were regular members. Sister Nancy
Grigsby had then come in with a "protest" that she was
"not satisfied with Brother and Sister Lincoln." The
trustees took back the letter, investigated, gave the letter
again to Brother and Sister Lincoln, and to show how they
felt about it, they appointed Brother Lincoln on a committee to straighten out a squabble between Sister Nancy
Grigsby and Sister Betsy Crawford. And it was jotted
down in the Pigeon church records and approved by the
trustees.

The ox wagon they made that winter was wood all
through, pegs, cleats, hickory withes, and knots of bark,
holding it together, except the wheel rims, which were
iron. Bundles of bed-clothes, skillets, ovens, and a few
pieces of furniture were loaded, stuck, filled and tied onto
the wagon; early one morning the last of the packing was

[203]

done. It was February 15, 1830; Abraham Lincoln had been four days a full-grown man, a citizen who "had reached his majority"; he could vote at elections from now on; he was lawfully free from his father's commands; he could come and go now; he was footloose.

At Jones's store he had laid in a little stock of pins, needles, buttons, tinware, suspenders, and knickknacks, to peddle on the way to Illinois.

And he had gone for a final look at the winter dry grass, the ruins of last year's wild vine and dogwood over the grave of Nancy Hanks. He and his father were leaving their Indiana home that day; almost naked they had come, stayed fourteen years, toiled, buried their dead, built a church, toiled on; and now they were leaving, almost naked. Now, with the women and children lifted on top of the wagon-load, the men walked alongside, curling and cracking their whip-lashes over the horns or into the hides of the half-broken young steers.

And so the seven-yoke team of young steers, each with his head in a massive collar of hardwood, lashed and bawled at with "Gee," "Haw," "G' lang" and "Hi thar, you! Git up!" hauled the lumbering pioneer load from the yellow and red clay of Spencer County, in southern Indiana, to the black loam of the prairie lands in Macon County, Illinois.

They had crossed the Wabash River, the state line of Illinois, and the Sangamo River, on a two-week trip with the ground freezing at night and thawing during the day, the steers slipping and tugging, the wagon axles groaning, the pegs and cleats squeaking. A dog was left behind one morning as the wagon crossed a stream; it whined, ran back and forth, but wouldn't jump in and swim across; young Lincoln took off boots and socks, waded into the icy water, gathered the hound in his arms and carried it over.

Near the Indiana-Illinois state line, Lincoln took his pack of needles and notions and walked up to a small farmhouse that seemed to him to be "full of nothing but children." They were of assorted sizes, seventeen months to seventeen years in age, and all in tears. The mother, red-headed and red-faced, clutched a whip in her fingers. The father, meek, mild, cow-headed, stood in the front doorway as if waiting for his turn to feel the thongs. Lincoln thought there wouldn't be much use in asking the woman if she wanted any needles and notions; she was busy, with a keen eye on the children and an occasional glance at her man in the doorway.

She saw Lincoln come up the path, stepped toward the door, pushed her husband out of the way, and asked Lincoln what was his business. "Nothing, madam," he answered gently, "I merely dropped in as I came along to see how things were going." He waited a moment.

"Well, you needn't wait," the woman snapped out. "There's trouble here, and lots of it, too, but I kin manage my own affairs without the help of outsiders. This is jest a family row, but I'll teach these brats their places ef I have to lick the hide off every one of 'em. I don't do much talkin' but I run this house, so I don't want no one sneakin' round tryin' to find out how I do it, either."

Around them as they crossed the first stretch of the Grand Prairie was a land and soil different from Indiana or Kentucky. There were long levels, running without slopes up or hollows down, straight to the horizon; arches and domes of sky covered it; the sky counted for more, seemed to have another language and way of talk, farther silences, too, than east and south where the new settlers had come from. Grass stood up six and eight feet; men and horses and cattle were lost to sight in it; so tough were the grass-roots that timber could not get rootholds in it; the grass seemed to be saying to the trees, "You shall not cross"; turf and sky had a new way of saying, "We are here—who are you?" to the ox-wagon gang hunting a new home.

Buffalo paths, deer tracks, were seen; coon, possum, and wolf signs were seen or heard. And they met settlers telling

"THIS IS JEST

A FAMILY ROW"

how the sod was so tough it had broken many a plow; but after the first year of sod-corn, the yield would run 50 bushels to the acre; wheat would average 25 to 30 bushels, rye the same, oats 40 to 60 bushels; Irish potatoes, timothy hay, and all the garden vegetables tried so far would grow. Horses and cattle, lean from short fodder through the winter, would fatten and shine with a gloss on their hair when turned loose in the wild grass in spring. Beds of wild strawberries came ripe in June and stained horses and cattle crimson to the knees. Wild horses and wild hogs were still to be found.

The outfit from Indiana raised a laugh as they drove their steers and wagon into the main street of Decatur, a county-seat settlement where court would hold its first session the coming May. To the question, "Kin ye tell us where John Hanks' place is?" the Decatur citizens told them how to drive four miles, where they found John, talked over old Indiana and Kentucky times, but more about Illinois. After the night stay, John took the Lincoln family six miles down the Sangamo River, where he had cut the logs for their cabin. There young Lincoln helped raise the cabin, put in the crops, split rails for fences. He hired out to Major Warnick near by, read the few books in the house, and passed such pleasant talk and smiles with the major's daughter, Mary, and with another girl, Jemima Hill, that at a later time neighbors said he carried on courtships, even though both girls married inside of a year after young Lincoln kept company in those parts. He was asking himself when he would get married, if ever.

He wrote back to Jones at Gentryville that he doubled his money on the peddler's stock he sold; he earned a pair of brown jean trousers by splitting four hundred rails for each yard of the cloth. With new outlooks came new thoughts; at Vincennes, on the way to Illinois, he had seen a printing-press for the first time, and a juggler who did sleight-of-hand tricks. John Hanks put him on a box to answer the speech of a man who was against improvements of the Sangamo River; and John told neighbors, "Abe beat him to death." More and more he was delivering speeches, to trees, stumps, potato rows, just practicing, by himself.

Fall came, with miasma rising from the prairie, and chills, fever, ague, for Tom Lincoln and Sally Bush, and many doses of "Barks," a Peruvian bark and whisky tonic mixture, bought at Renshaw's general store in Decatur. Then came Indian summer, and soft weather, till Christmas week. And then a snowstorm.

For forty-eight hours, with no let-up, the battalions of a blizzard filled the sky, and piled a cover two and a half feet deep on the ground. No sooner was this packed down and frozen than another drive of snow came till there was a four-foot depth of it on the level. It was easy picking for the light-footed wolves who could run on the top crust and take their way with cattle. Wheat crops went to ruin; cows, hogs, horses died in the fields. Connections between houses, settlements, grain mills, broke down; for days families were cut off, living on parched corn; some died of cold, lacking wood to burn; some died of hunger lacking corn.

Those who came through alive, in the years after, called themselves "Snowbirds." The Lincoln family had hard days. It was hard on new settlers with no reserve stocks of meat, corn, and wood; young Lincoln made a try at wading through to the Warnick house four miles off, nearly froze his feet, and was laid up at home.

As the winter eased off, the Lincoln family moved southeast a hundred miles to Goose Nest Prairie, in the southern part of Coles County.

CHAPTER XXVI

EIGHT miles from the new farm was the town of Charleston. Young Lincoln drove there with an ox team and sold loads of cordwood split with his own ax. One afternoon he was late in selling his wood and decided with dark coming on he wouldn't try to drive his ox team to the farm. Tarlton Miles, the horse doctor, living just outside of Charleston, took him in overnight, and they sat up till midnight talking.

In the morning, Lincoln goaded his steers on out to the farm, drove wedges with a maul, split more cordwood. In the evening, as he lay on a board reading, a stranger came to the house and asked to stay overnight. Tom Lincoln said there were only two beds, one belonged to his son, and it depended on whether his son wanted to sleep with a stranger. The two shared the bed that night. . . . It was a country where the veterinary surgeon took in the ox-driver and the ox-driver took in the stranger.

Over in Cumberland County, which joined Coles, the champion wrestler was Dan Needham. It came to his ears several times that the new tall boy over at Goose Nest could throw him. "I can fling him three best out of four any day," was Needham's answer. At a house-raising at Wabash Point the two faced each other, each one standing six feet, four inches, each a prairie panther. "Abe, rassle 'im," said Tom Lincoln.

Abe held off; the crowd egged both of them on. They grappled four times and each time Needham went under. Then Needham lost his head, threatened a fist fight, calmed down with hearing Lincoln's drawling banter, and at last put out his hand with a grin and said, "Well, I'll be damned." And they shook hands.

In February, 1831, there came to the neighborhood of John Hanks, when Abe Lincoln was lingering there, a man named Denton Offut, a hard drinker, a hustler, and a talker shrewd with his tongue, easy with promises, a believer in pots of gold at the rainbow end. He would have a flatboat and cargo to go to New Orleans, all ready for Abe Lincoln, John Hanks, and John Johnston, "as soon as the snow should go off," if they would meet him on a Sangamo River branch near the village of Springfield. They were there at the time set but Denton Offut wasn't; they walked to Springfield, asked for Offut, found him drunk at the Buckhorn Tavern, and helped sober him.

Offut hired them at twelve dollars a month, gave them permission to go onto Government timber-land and get out gunwales for the flatboat, while the rest of the needed lumber could come from Kirkpatrick's sawmill, charged to Offut. They slung together a camp outfit and started building, with Lincoln calling himself "chief cook and bottle-washer." A sleight-of-hand performer came along and giving his show asked for an empty hat to take eggs out of. Lincoln offered his hat in a hesitating way, saying he hesitated not so much out of respect for the hat as for the eggs.

Two men whose canoe turned over and got away from them were shivering in a tree on a raw April day with the freshet-flooded Sangamo River under them. Lincoln got out across the rampaging waters to the tree, on a log with a rope tied to it; the men in the tree straddled the log and were pulled on shore. People began talking about Lincoln's cool wit.

Thirty days saw the flatboat finished, loaded, and on her way, with Lincoln on deck in blue homespun jeans, jacket, vest, rawhide boots with pantaloons stuffed in, and a felt hat once black but now, as the owner said, "sunburned till it was a combine of colors." On April 19, rounding the curve of the Sangamo at the village of New Salem, the boat stuck on the Cameron mill-dam, and hung with one third of her slanted downward over the edge of the dam and filling slowly with water, while the cargo of pork-barrels was sliding slowly so as to overweight one end.

She hung there a day while all the people of New Salem came down to look at the river disaster, which Lincoln fixed by unloading the pork barrels into another boat, boring a hole in the end of the flatboat as it hung over the dam, letting the water out, dropping the boat over the dam and reloading. As she headed toward the Mississippi watercourse, New Salem talked about the cool head and ready wit of the long-shanked young man with his pantaloons stuffed in his rawhide boots.

Again Lincoln floated down the Mississippi River, four to six miles an hour, meeting strings of other flatboats, keel-boats, arks, sleds, proud white steamboats flying flags. Stepping off their flatboat at New Orleans, Lincoln and Hanks went nearly a mile, walking on flatboats, to reach shore. Stacks of pork and flour from the West, and piles of cotton bales from the South, stood on the wharves. Some shippers, about one in six, were cursing their luck; on the long haul from north of the Ohio River their pork and flour had spoiled; all they got for their trip was the view of the Mississippi River scenery. In New Orleans, Lincoln saw advertisements of traders offering to "pay the highest prices in cash for good and likely Negroes" or to "attend to the sale and purchase of Negroes on commission." A firm advertised: "We have now on hand, and intend to keep throughout the entire year, a large and well-selected stock of Negroes, consisting of field hands, house servants, mechanics, cooks, seamstresses, washers, ironers, etc., which we can sell and will sell as low or lower than any other house here or in New Orleans; persons wishing to purchase would do well to call on us before making purchases elsewhere, as our fresh and regular arrivals will keep us supplied with a good and general assortment; our terms are liberal; give us a call."

One trader gave notice: "I will at all times pay the highest cash prices for Negroes of every description, and will also attend to the sale of Negroes on commission, having a jail and yard fitted up expressly for boarding them." Another announced: "The undersigned would respectfully state to the public that he has forty-five Negroes now on hand, having this day received a lot of twenty-five direct from Virginia, two or three good cooks, a carriage driver, a good house boy, a fiddler, a fine seamstress, and a likely lot of field men and women; all of whom he will sell at a

SLAVE MARKET

small profit; he wishes to close out and go on to Virginia after a lot for the fall trade." There were sellers advertising, "For sale—several likely girls from 10 to 18 years old, a woman 24, a very valuable woman 25, with three very likely children," while buyers indicated wants after the manner of one advertising, "Wanted—I want to purchase twenty-five likely Negroes, between the ages of 18 and 25 years, male and female, for which I will pay the highest prices in cash."

An Alabama planter advertised, "Runaway—Alfred, a bright mulatto boy, working on plantation; about 18 years old, pretty well grown, has blue eyes, light flaxen hair, skin disposed to freckles; he will try to pass as free-born." Another Alabama planter gave notice: "One hundred dollars reward for return of a bright mulatto man slave, named Sam; light sandy hair, blue eyes, ruddy complexion, is so white as very easily to pass for a free white man."

Lincoln saw one auction in New Orleans where an octoroon girl was sold, after being pinched, trotted up and down, and handled so the buyer could be satisfied she was sound of wind and limb. After a month's stay he worked his passage, firing a steamboat furnace, up the Mississippi River, stayed a few weeks on his father's farm in Coles County, Illinois, and then spoke the long good-by to home and the family roof.

Saying good-by to his father was easy, but it was not so easy to hug the mother, Sally Bush, and put his long arms around her, and lay his cheeks next to hers and say he was going out into the big world to make a place for himself.

The father laughed his good-by, and not so long after told a visitor: "I s'pose Abe is still fooling hisself with eddication. I tried to stop it, but he has got that fool idea in his head, and it can't be got out. Now I hain't got no eddication, but I get along far better'n ef I had. Take bookkeepin'—why, I'm the best bookkeeper in the world! Look up at that rafter thar. Thar's three straight lines made with a firebrand: ef I sell a peck of meal I draw a black line across, and when they pay, I take a dishcloth and jest rub it out; and that thar's a heap better'n yer eddication." And the visitor who heard this told friends that Thomas Lincoln was "one of the shrewdest ignorant men" he had ever seen.

With his few belongings wrapped in a handkerchief bundle tied to a stick over his shoulder, Abraham was on his way to New Salem.